SO THERE I WAS . . .

Peggy Senger Parsons

SO THERE I WAS ...

Copyright © 2009 by Peggy Senger Parsons

The cover photo is by Alivia Biko

Scripture Quotes: Old Testament quotes are King James Version, New Testament quotes are Peggy Parsons' own translation or paraphrases from the original.

Contents

6

Foreword

I have been telling stories for as long as I can remember. My reputation predates my memory. Some people in my family considered it prevarication. I now consider it a stage in the formation of a narrative theologian. Sounds better, no? I began writing stories when all I had at my disposal were Crayolas. In the middle grades I fell for Ambrose Bierce and O. Henry, and the columnists in the three Chicago newspapers.

I tried writing about other people, and imaginary people, but always came back to the Midrash of my own existence. I thought this to be a bit narcissistic for a bit. But I thought better of this on the advice of two excellent sources, Alcoholics Anonymous and George Fox, founder of Quakerism. AA says that the only thing you have to give is your own hope and experience. Nothing else is authentic. AA is a fine religion. George said that in service of the truth we should "Let all nations hear the sound by word or writing. Spare no place, spare no tongue or pen, but be obedient to the Lord God; go through the work, be valiant for the truth upon the earth; and tread and trample down what is contrary." Old School moxie – that guy. He added to that, "Be patterns, be examples in all countries, places, islands, nations wherever you come; that your carriage and life may preach among all sorts of people." So I use my life as the teaching example. Not because I think it is all that special, but it is the only life I have to speak of. And paradoxically, as I use my life to talk about the things of God, my life becomes less about me.

My willingness to use my life and have my life used does seem to have increased the quantity and quality of interesting experiences. Black preachers have a call they are fond of -- "I need a witness!" I have found that I am often grateful for the witnesses to my life. For the record, the stories in this book are completely non-fiction.

The following columns are sixty of a hundred that I wrote for the United Press International's Religion and Spirituality Forum between January 2006 and March 2008. I expect to publish the others, and new ones, in volumes to follow.

I will always be grateful to Pamela Calvert for forwarding me the email calling for writers, and for my editor at UPI Larry Moffitt who helped me find the courage to defend my voice and my words. Gratitude to all the readers of my blog for giving me hope that someone would want to buy this book. Gratitude to my daughters for keeping me honest. Nothing in my life would work right without Alivia Biko.

This is dedicated to Nia Grace Cline, who will know her grandmother's stories.

Spiritual Disciplines for the 21st Century

Practice may not always make perfect, but the correlation between practice and progress is extremely high. A long time ago I decided that I did not want to eat at a spiritual smorgasbord. I wanted to choose a path and take it as far as I could. I am a Christian, and after that I am a Quaker. But choosing my path was the smallest part of the job. Exercising my soul, like exercising my body, is an unending discipline. The following columns describe my exercise routine. I can attest to results in direct relation to effort.

Adventure

So there I was ...

halfway across the state of Texas working on a spiritual discipline.

I am mildly allergic to the entire concept of discipline. It smacks of work. It stinks of tedium. These things do not call to me. But I do desire to be a deeply spiritual person. Not the kind of pop-faith consumer who has a new guru or path with every season. I am ready to settle down: to choose one path and stick to it, and spend the second half of my life mastering it. To do this, I am afraid that I must practice a spiritual discipline or two.

The purpose of practicing any spiritual discipline is twofold: to aerobically exercise the soul and to increase awareness of the Divine. The traditional practices of prayer, fasting, simplicity, and so on, have great merit, and I occasionally work at them. But I have found a new discipline that suits me, and stretches me in ways I never thought possible. It is the Discipline of Spiritual Adventure.

The Discipline of Spiritual Adventure is not just simple thrill seeking, but the intentional choosing of the less certain way in order to allow the Divine maximum room to move. When we are outside of our comfort zone, when we are on an unknown path, our senses are heightened, including our spiritual senses that so often lay dormant as we proceed through life on autopilot. On an adventure we pay more attention to detail. We are aware of, and communicate our thoughts and desires, more diligently to our Designer. We listen better.

Choice is an essential piece of spiritual adventure. We must acknowledge, embrace, and take responsibility for the freedom we are given as eternal children of a Divine Creator. An adventure that is not freely chosen is a detour at best, and sometimes a nightmare. Many of us use our freedom to so fill our lives with busyness, structure, and control that there is no room for adventure. We do this almost without thinking, unconsciously barricading our life against the unknown. But I tell you, it is still choice; it is intentional, and intention counts.

It is not a spiritual adventure if you are treading a well-worn path. Fresh road is required: navigating not by memory, but by a combination of reason and trust. You must become aware of crossroads when you come to them. Often they are not marked or obvious. Daily we make decisions that will change our entire future; often it is only in hindsight that we see it. The discipline of spiritual adventure says that we can develop foresight and a present awareness that allows us to be fully conscious participants in our choices. And beyond that, it tells us that the universe is trustworthy and that we can renounce fear, and trust our Creator and our own spiritual senses to keep us away from real disaster when on uncertain paths. A crossroads is a pivotal place where fear wrestles with obedience. It is one of the best places I know of to develop discernment, or wisdom listening.

But we do not seek this discipline purposeless; we seek it with the desire, the craving, to see with our own eyes the movement, influence, and evidence of the Divine. We can only see this when we get our plans, agendas, and ourselves out of the way. There are no preplanned spaces in my Day-Timer for miracles.

Spiritual adventure can be fun, but often it isn't. It is always stretching. Even a genuine miracle can be scary at the time -- just ask Jonah. It doesn't always feel safe, but practiced properly, it is safe. In fact, it is much safer than living a spiritually unaware, unawakened life.

Simple risk taking is betting on your luck, or your skill; like any bet the odds can be good, or the shot can be a long one. Spiritual adventure presumes that there is another player, and that the Other has your true best interests as its goal and guiding principle. This is an essential truth: yes, the house always wins, but you and the house have intimate connections.

When we walk in expectant, holy boldness, we are alive to the moment, holding only the ground we stand on, ceding all else to possibility. Divinity loves this. It makes excellent dance partners of us, and Divinity loves to dance. Often Divinity leads, but It enjoys just being with us, and lets us lead if we wish. Divinity loves to protect and to play. At times, Divinity loves to party.

So that is how I got to a spiritual crossroads in the middle of Texas. I was on a cross-country motorcycle ride and it was a spiritual adventure. I had planned my trip as carefully as a human can plan. But I also had learned to trust the unexpected, and listen for the voice of the Divine coming from strange quarters.

On a day that the weatherman predicted to be clear and warm for the entire state, I encountered divine providence in the words of an unusually bold stranger. I had stopped for gas at a town aptly named "Junction." Sitting on the porch of the gas station was an old lady, nursing a soda in the afternoon heat. She watched me pump gas, she watched me pay for gas, and just as I was getting ready to leave she said:

"Where y'all goin?"

"Up to Sweetwater via Abilene."

"Fixin' to take the highway?"

"Yes ma'am, straight north from here."

"Don't."

"Excuse me?"

"You don't want to go that way -- you want to go up the back way through Eden and San Angelo."

(Generally speaking, I don't care for people telling me what I want and don't want.)

"But my map shows the road through Abilene to be shorter."

"You deaf? (Pronounced deef) Or are you just not listenin', girl?"

"Is there construction, or something I don't know about on the road to Abilene?"

"You're kinda' stubborn, ain'tcha? Or maybe you're just not a bright chile? You do as I tell you, ya hear?"

"Yes Ma'am - Thank-you."

She just wasn't the kind of lady that you argued with and expected to win. I decided to follow her advice. The roads she put me on were smaller, and longer, but all went well. About halfway north I did notice some black storm clouds off to my right, but the sun shone on me the whole way. At last I pulled into Sweetwater and got a room. I turned the TV on in time to see a news report that Abilene had gotten hit by a freak thunderstorm that afternoon; they had 6 inches of rain, flash flooding, golf-ball sized hail and two tornado cells. All of this directly on the route I had planned, and because of "Our Lady of Junction," all precisely one county east of me.

When you have choices to make, does it seem at times that Wisdom is silent? Does this frustrate you? Cause you to be afraid? Confuse you? I would ask you first, if you have had a time in the past when the right choice and true path was clear. If you do, then you can rest confidently in the knowledge that if it was important for you to choose one way over the other, that Wisdom will show up. If you do not feel that clear direction, then be happy! You may be facing the prospect of Spiritual Adventure. Choose the less certain way this time. Listen to the crazy stranger. Make the expressed intention of your heart to make the most room for the

Divine to move. Then proceed, with alert attention, listening ears, and a light step. Watch and see the handiwork of the Sacred. Miracles may happen, strangers will speak truth, and angels will become your comrades. And you will grow - I guarantee it.

Attendance

So there I was ...

driving away from my house on a busy Monday morning. My "To Do" list was stacked like planes coming into O'Hare. My head was in air traffic control mode, oblivious to everything but the blips on my personal radar.

I slowed to a not-quite-full-legal stop at the corner of My Street and Major Arterial. The bank was cleared for landing and the post-office was on final approach. Then that still small voice I have learned to listen to piped up with an urgent request.

"Peggy, could you please attend to the train coming into Grand Central Station on track number Four? – it's coming in a little fast."

"Whaaa?"

I applied full brake and looked about. All seemed normal in the sleepy residential neighborhood. Then I saw her: the little choo-choo on track number Four. She was about two years old – maybe – riding a big wheel along Major Arterial. She was blonde, female, (probably) and peddling along at good speed, about a block and a half away. With no adult anywhere in sight. I parked. She peddled towards me, crossed the next side street at below bumper height, and kept coming. She never looked sideways or back. I got out and met her on the sidewalk. She applied her Fred Flintstones and came to a stop at my toes.

"Hi baby."

She looked up at me and put her thumb in her mouth.

"Baby, where's Mommy?"

Tot unplugged thumb and looked over her shoulder.

"Let's go find Mommy, ok?"

"Otay." she chirped.

Executing a crisp three-point Big Wheel turn, Cindy Lou Who applied speed and proceeded in the direction of her origin. I followed at a brisk walking pace.

We went three full city blocks, crossing two side streets, this time with me as crossing guard, and then she made a right turn. I was about to call 911 when a door opened at the end of the block and a blonde woman popped out her head and called, "Haley?"

I continued to Haley's house. I informed Mom of where I had contacted Haley. Mom thanked me and was about to start scolding Haley. As a card-carrying member and journeywoman of the International Union of Mothers, I felt the need to interrupt and make the lesson explicit.

"I could have as easily picked her up and put her in my car." I said gently.

Mom looked a little stunned.

"It's not Haley's job to keep Haley safe." I said even more gently.

Mom scooped Haley up in her arms and nodded.

"Have a good day. Bye, Haley."

"Bye-Bye." chirped the tot.

I returned to my car and to my radar.

This was not an unusual occurrence in my life. My children could tell you how young they were when they noticed that their mother seemed to be "on call" to the universe. My therapist might tell you that I have rescuing tendencies. I prefer to say that I practice the Spiritual Discipline of Attendance. The Biblical mandate for this is the story Jesus told about the guy in the ditch. Of course, it is more formally known as "The Story of the Guy Who Helped the Guy in the Ditch," but you know the story. It's all about looking off your own radar and showing up where you are needed when you are needed and then taking action.

Here are the requirements of the Spiritual Discipline of Attendance:

You must attend.

You must be able to be present and mindful; aware of your surroundings. You must be able to observe without seeking to simply fit what you observe into your ready-made boxes

You must attend at two levels. You must be able to have one ear and eye on the world and one ear and eye on the Divine. You must be willing to take input from the Divine. This is what makes it a spiritual discipline and not merely paying attention – which is not a bad thing – but is different.

You must attend with the expectation of use.

You must show up for life willing to take action. You accept the fact that in any given situation you may be the person most capable of attendance.

You must attend with minimum fear. Sometimes all you have to offer is a non-anxious presence. Sometimes you may be called upon to be resilient in the face of actual threat. Fear kills love and a lot of other things.

You must attend with hope. Ditch people can't always dredge up their own. You must carry a supply of this at all times.

You must attend with Faith. (See above) Sometimes people have to be able to believe in you before they can believe in anything else. It takes courage and integrity to put yourself out there. If you try and attend without faith in yourself, and in a power greater than yourself, you will incinerate quickly.

You must attend with Love. (See above) It is advisable to carry as much of this as possible, and to stock up at every opportunity. You cannot top the tank too often.

You must attend without entanglement. You must have a healthy sense of self in order to keep yourself out of the ditch. Never think that you are too cool to fall into a ditch. Ditches are sneaky. You must not attempt to do for people what they can and should do for themselves.

The guy who helped the guy in the ditch was able to do some very personal attendance, and then he delegated.

Now, finally, to make the lesson explicit, **this is not an optional discipline**. Evil also attends, with diligence and willingness. Evil carries a stockpile of strife, malice, and despair. Evil wants you to think that it is bold and fearless, but evil is actually reckless out of necessity because evil is afraid, very, very afraid. Afraid, among other things, that we will all learn to attend.

The Story of the Guy Who Helped the Guy in the Ditch is found in the book of Luke, the 10th chapter, in the Christian New Testament.

Compassion

So there I was ...

in an airport concourse so long I could see the curvature of the Earth. Gate B-95, no kidding. Deep winter, northern Europe, holiday season – Delay Central.

I was still pretty fresh when she caught my eye. Mid-twenties, with a baby at her breast, four pieces of luggage, a half-crazed two-year-old boy and a compelling look of desperation.

Life presented me with about three seconds to make a decision. Look the other way, or be drawn into a vortex of need.

Compassion struck and I surrendered to it. I am a fairly high-ranking member of the International Union of Mothers, and there are rules about these things.

I engaged the toddler, and then took the well-fed babe for a sleep in my arms, while the mother changed the boy's diaper and rearranged herself and her luggage. She was on her way to Copenhagen from Vancouver, British Columbia - she had experienced two delays already. She wanted to see her parents. Women will do crazy things for love.

The most important thing I did was make sane adult conversation with an intelligent young woman at her wit's end. You can give people some of your wits when they have exhausted theirs –wits transfer - Wits R Us – this is good.

She needed to see a ticket agent. She looked at me, took a deep breath, and made a huge decision. She decided to trust. It was a stunning act of beauty in an airport, our high temples of fear-driven security. A wave of warmth spread out from her and the anxious people around her shuddered a bit as the scent of Heaven massaged their tight spots. Angels whistled low and long.

"I am going to take the boy and see the agent; can I leave the luggage and the baby with you?"

I looked her in the soul and spoke with gentle authority.

"She is safe here – All is well – do what you need to do."

"You have no idea how I appreciate this."

"Actually, I do; been here, done this."

An hour later I walked them to their gate and saw them on their way.

Compassion is a mystery. It is like unto its sisters, Love and Forgiveness. It has a big emotional component; sometimes it just falls upon you.

Compassion also requires action. Without action, the feeling is called pity, and there are really good reasons that everyone disdains pity.

It is also a decision; you always have the choice to look the other way. Some days you assess the need of the other, and of yourself, and realize that you have to take

care of yourself. You may determine that your resources and the need at hand are not a good match.
You may realize that the need is too big and that the
best you can do is report the situation to the switch-
board at Higher Power Inc. They dispatch 24/7.

Compassion is an emotional, decisive, course of action.
Thank God, it is as common as dirt. And it is also one of
the most powerful agents working in our world. It is an
essential spiritual discipline.

Mix it with a little trust and the gates of Hell get
rattled.

Courage

So there I was ...

teaching trauma healing to my first group of African students. They were women and men, old and young, Catholic and Quaker, highly or barely educated. The one thing they had in common was a deep desire to learn how to bring healing from the horror that was all around them in Burundi, a country that had survived ten years of war and genocide.

I had the latest theory and methods on treating Post-Traumatic Stress Disorder in my back pocket. I was an experienced teacher, but I had not one word of language in common with them. I was to teach six hours a day, five days a week for two weeks. I thought I was brave to come all this way and give it a try.

I was assigned a team of translators. I worked them so hard that I used them in tag team fashion. Kirundi is not a language conducive to psychobabble, so I was working at simplifying my language, and I tried to jettison the jargon unless it was critical. Yet my translator would often hold up a hand to stop me and there would be an animated discussion in Kirundi and sometimes French until they coined a new word – at which point my translator would say "Voila!" and we would proceed. We had one aide de camp assigned to write these words down and we generated a Kirundi glossary of psychological terms. I felt very successful.

Our second morning, there was what my Burundian friends euphemistically call "activity" outside the compound. All I heard was a small thump and a tapping noise – I thought someone was moving furniture and hanging pictures until I noticed that every one of my 14 students had a stiff body, glazed eyes and did not appear to be breathing. A few seconds of silence later, my translator whispered "Mambo sawa" (Kiswahili for things are ok) and as one, they shuddered and came back to the here and now. It turns out that the noise I heard was a hand grenade and some automatic rifle fire, at a not-far-enough distance. That was when I decided to administer a PTSD checklist to my students and found out that all my healers were in need of healing.

The third morning I was relaxing enough in my teaching to start noticing details about individual students. Jerson had only one ear. At break I put my hand to his head and made universal female clucking sounds of sympathy. "Machete" said Jerson with a smile on his face.

Ernest had one hand in a large bandage. I noticed something else about Ernest. He often started taking notes in the space between my speaking and the translator's. I suspected he had more English than he was letting on. I was sure of it when I made a lame attempt at a joke, and he laughed at the tag of my punch line, and all the other students looked at him and then looked expectantly at the translator for their funny. At lunch I got him aside without an intermediary and said "Ernest, you are such a bright student – where did you get your English?"

He looked at me. Sized me up. Made a decision. And then, out came the story of Ernest Toyi, Greatheart.

Ernest hailed from the town of Makamba, almost on the border of Tanzania. Several long, awful, bus rides from the capital. He was always a studious child, eager for learning. He got a start on English in secondary school, but the war interrupted his studies. His town was squarely in the middle of rebel control. Life was hard. The rebels were suspicious of education and extremely suspicious of outsiders. Ernest had a long-standing habit of attempting to speak with anyone who had English, in order to improve his own.

He came to the attention of the local leaders for doing just that, speaking English to someone from the outside. They hauled him in and interrogated him, when that produced nothing, they tortured him by bending his thumbs back and burning him between his fingers with a cigarette. This also got them nothing, so they tossed him in the street and figured they had taught him a lesson.

Ernest bandaged his hand and a few days later he met with someone from the local Trauma Healing Center. They recognized promise in Ernest and recommended him for the classes that were about to be held in the capital. And so Ernest the Brave and his tortured hand left to go and learn from an English-speaking teacher in the enemy capital.

Ernest was my best student of that batch. He studied at night and asked me tough questions by day. He was curious, skeptical and eager. When we finished, the director of the Trauma Healing Organization asked me whom I thought he should hire for the Makamba center. I had no trouble nominating Ernest.

Ernest the Courageous went back to rebel-held Makamba. He worked to heal others. His courage, giftedness, and diligence did not go unnoticed. When the war was over, he ran for local office and was eventually elected Chief of Zone – something like Mayor of Makamba. I have every reason to hope and believe that they do not torture people there on the watch of Ernest Toyi.

Thus did I learn the Spiritual Discipline of Courage from one of its masters. Courage knows fear and walks right through it. Courage is friends with hard work. Courage has a purpose that reckless and thrill-seeking will never know. Courage does not step out from great riches to risk the tithe. Courage pays the price upfront with a promise made from faith and hope. Courage walks the path of righteousness and counts on the vouchsafe of God. Courage counts the coup before the battle begins, and accepts its own wounds as the proof of honor. Courage can never be foresworn.

I pray that someday, I will be honored enough of God to be given the chance to be courageous. I pray that the teacher is worthy of her students.

(I spent three months in 2003 working in Burundi, Central Africa for THARS.org)

Failure

So there I was ...

at the Department of Motor Vehicles taking the motor-cycle endorsement test for the first time. As a permitted learner, but not a licensed rider, I had arrived accompanied by an experienced rider.

Just like with cars, you can practice riding on the streets with an experienced friend. Unlike practice driving in a car, if you make a big mistake, all your friend on the other bike can do is scream and then call 911.

My friend Owen had not only taught me how to ride, he had financed my first bike. He is that sort of a friend. That day he stood on the sidelines and watched as I went through my paces on my shiny new Honda Rebel. At 250 cc's and a mere 300 lbs., she was just the light, nimble bike that you wanted for the test.

They do this test off road, in a parking lot that is painted with a test course. The tester that day was a serious looking young man with a clipboard. He inspected my bike and my gear, gave me instructions and then the go-ahead. I did great at the slalom cones. I braked from speed without skidding. I demonstrated the ability to use turn signals and horns without problem, downshifted on a corner. I passed all his tasks with ease until the last one. This was the "tight turn trick." Painted on the pavement was a three-sided bay - precisely the size of two parking spaces. You were required to enter on the left side going at least 15 mph, you must then execute a turn inside this bay and exit on the right side without touching the white lines. There was a dot painted at the apex for reference. I had practiced a U-turn on a two-lane road, but this was considerably tighter. I gave it my best shot. Gas to 15. Entered bay. Braked. Turned at apex. Made a critical mistake. I looked down at the dot on the pavement, and then the bike was down, and I was standing over her. I looked up. Owen had his eyes covered, cringing. The clipboard boy was shaking his head and walking towards me.

I was furious and humiliated.

I don't remember picking up my bike. The next thing I do remember was putting the front wheel back down on the ground from somewhere in mid air. Apparently I was pumping a bit of adrenaline. I remember the front tire bouncing as I set it back down. I looked up again at the clipboard guy. He stopped, took one step backward, and made a "settle down" gesture with his free hand – eyes wide open.

"Ma'am, you ok?"

"Grrr – I flunked – right?"

"You are going to have to wait three days to take the test again – but you can take it again – I am sure you will pass next time – ma'am."

"Grrr."

Guy to Owen: "Make sure she takes a few minutes to calm down before you guys ride home, ok?"

I did calm down, a bit. The fury wore off with the stress hormones. But I was in complete freak-out about flunking. I just could not believe it. I called a sympathetic friend.

"I flunked! I can't believe it. I flunked!"

"Peggy, chill, it's just like flunking a quiz at school, only with infinite do-overs."

"Excuse **me**! I have **never** flunked a quiz."

"Never? Never in 20 years of school?"

"Of course not!"

"Um, Ok – it's like getting fired from a job – you get another job."

"Oh, give me a break –**no one** has ever fired **me**."

"Man ... then it is like getting dumped."

"What!? Dumped? I don't think so!"

"You know what, Peggy? You needed this – God decided it was your turn."

My friend was right. I was in a failure deficit situation, and that is not good. I was 35 years old and I had never learned the Spiritual Discipline of Failure. This is not an optional discipline. And as it turned out in the next decade of my life I was going to be in a couple of big situations where success by any normal standard of success was not going to be possible, and God needed me to be fit for the task. So I started a series of practicums in the art of not getting it anything close to right.

It's a tough class.

The core truth of this discipline is that you must learn to take your focus off of "outcome" and put it onto "process." I had been hung up on flunking and not looking at how I flunked. This is a killer of a mistake. It not only can get you killed in certain situations, it kills learning and joy the rest of the time. It drastically increases fear because there is always a dreaded outcome and never a preventative within your control. I needed to forget about the test, and learn the crucial lesson that motorcycles will go wherever you put your eyes. In a tight turn you look out to your exit, not down at the pavement. When you learn this lesson, tight turns cease to be scary. And Friends, Life offers many opportunities for the quick u-turn.

I don't really see God as some sort of cosmic tester with a clipboard, but I have learned to leave the outcomes up to God. When faced with an experience that looks like failure, I take a deep breath, calm down, and look at what I am doing; inevitably there is a part of the situation that I am trying to control that was really not in my power, and part of the situation that actually was in my control that I was ignoring or didn't recognize. Then I let go of the former, focus on the latter and sign up for do-overs.

Fortunately for me, I worship a God of infinite do-overs.

Forgiveness

So there I was ...

in a new house, trying to get to know my new neighbor. This old fellow was 96 years old, in relatively good health, living independently in his home. Besides always hoping to be a good neighbor, I am a collector of stories and I saw him as a potential treasure house of material.

I made a few advances, brought over leftovers, and started engaging in over-the-fence conversation. This was a man who should have remembered the turn of the 20th century, should have remembered not only the First World War, but also the Spanish American War. He should have remembered Shoeless Joe Jackson and the Black Socks scandal. But I soon found out that this old gent had only one story, a list of nine decades of offenses the world had dealt him. If you listened long enough the story always came back to a beating with a buggy whip that his father gave him as a boy for a bit of petty larceny that he did not commit – It was the injustice that started a life of injustice-list keeping. He had no other stories; it took too much energy to keep his list.

After failing to draw out any other story, I attempted to talk to him about a Galilean I knew who was also whipped for crimes uncommitted, but who managed to ask his father to forgive the abusers. When I used the word forgiveness, he gave me an odd look; as if it was a word he hadn't heard for a long time. He fell silent for a moment and then with sudden passion said,

"Forgiveness, huh? – When my old man was dying, he asked me to forgive him so he could die in peace. And I spat in his face and said 'You can rot in Hell for all eternity if my forgiveness is what you need!' I will never forgive that old man!"

My neighbor died just before his 100th birthday, un-changed, as far as I knew. I think it was as sad a situation as I have ever known - and completely preventable. I wonder if he knew the old proverb, "He who seeks revenge should dig two graves."

The Apostle Paul says this, in his letter to the Ephesians,

Let all bitterness, anger, uproar, and blasphemy with all their evil, be removed from you. Instead, become kind and tenderhearted to each other, forgiving each other in the same way that God through Christ forgave you. Then you will be imitators of God, Acting like beloved children. (Ephesians 4:25)

Here's what I notice about this counsel. First, that anger is a given, Paul wastes no time figuring out why it is there, it just is. Second, there is a process, not an event that is clearly injurious to the soul; anger turns to bitterness, which turns to uproar, which leads to blasphemy. Then there is another process described that is soul-nourishing, where anger leads to right choices, which leads to compassion which leads to forgiveness. It looks like the question is not how quick you forgive, or even if you get to the end of the process, but which road you are on. It seems that the essential key to resolution is direction.

Some people want forgiveness to be a simple choice, a decision. Some want it to be an emotion - if you feel like forgiving, great but, if not, don't worry – there are no bad feelings. Some want it to be an action you can take whether or not you believe it or feel like it – act like you forgive and maybe the other things will come along. I think that each of these is inadequate.

So what is it then? What is this thing we call forgiveness? I may not be able to name it, I may have to settle for just calling it a mystery, but I can recognize another member of its genus. It is like Love, which is also purported to be choice, feeling or behavior, but is in fact, in its pure form, a perfect integration of the three. Forgiveness is like this, a passionate, decisive course of action.

Passionate, because it clearly requires and emotional capacity. If you aren't ready, you just aren't ready. Decisive, because it is a choice available to a free soul, it is not a commandment. And a course of action, because it has to be lived out.

It's like driving a car to a certain destination. The cognitive part is deciding to make the trip and choosing the destination. This requires that you have knowledge of where you are going or the ability to read a map. And like any destination, if you have been there a few times, it gets easy to find again. It also requires that you look out of the windshield and assess information as you go. You must think all the way.

The emotional part is like the dashboard full of little lights that tell you if you are running hot or cold, if you have enough fuel etc. We all have emotional warning lights within us if we learn to pay attention to them.

The behavioral part is expressed by the fact that you have to actually do things; start the car, steer, brake etc. if you want to get to your destination.

Any of these parts can cause problems if you try to do without them. If you try to drive without gas or oil, and ignore the lights, you will fail. If you gas up but never look at a map or even look out the windshield, you will certainly not arrive at your destination. And if you plan, map, gas up but just sit there you will fail again. All systems must be go; all systems must cooperate together to get you to your destination.

So it is with forgiveness. If you decide to forgive, but ignore your emotional responses, your journey will be short. If you run entirely on emotions, and do not think or choose, your journey will be even shorter. And if you plan for the destination, and care for yourself, but do not enact your plan, it will be futile.

You must decide that you want to be on the road to forgiveness, even if it takes your whole life to pursue it. You must know what it looks like and what it will require of you. Then you must assess your own emotional capability. Filling as many deficits as you can, and doing careful self-nourishment along the way. You can also ask others skilled in the journey to offer guidance and care. It is also important to note that you need divine help in this. Paul noted that we were to let these things be removed from us. We choose to be helped on this journey. Forgiveness must come from a position of strength. The journey will take as long as it will take. I believe the length of time will be proportionate to the hurt. For small hurts, this process can be as short as a thought, a feeling, and an action in short succession, almost automatic. For the great injuries of life, this may be a long road, but it is infinitely better than the road of bitterness.

I read a quote* in a book by Joan Chittister, a prayer which she says was found by the body of a dead child at the Ravensbruck Concentration camp. I look at it now and then, not as a standard to be measured against, but as an inspiration.

"O Lord, remember not only the men and women of good will, but also those of ill will. But do not remember the suffering that they have inflicted upon us; remember rather the fruits that we have borne, thanks to the suffering - our comradeship, our loyalty, our humility, our courage, our generosity, the greatness of heart, which has grown out of all this, and when they come to judgment, let all the fruits we have borne be their forgiveness."

*Joan Chittister, *In Search of Belief* (Liguori, Missouri: Liguori/Triumph, 2006) pp. 189-190

Generosity

So there I was ...

on Saturday night, most nights of my childhood. Freshly scrubbed out of the tub, my Sunday school lesson book had no empty blanks. Sunday school came with homework back then. Mother was in the kitchen cranking off the church bulletins on the mimeograph machine – kachunk, kachunk, kachunk. Dad was in the living room ready to hand out weekly allowances to his progeny.

My allotment was one US dollar, and I got it whether I was naughty or nice – it was grace. But I received this allowance on Saturday evening for a specific purpose and in a specific form. I was given ten shiny dimes, after the candy store at the corner closed, when there was no other opportunity to spend my riches until Monday. I received it in dimes, not quarters, because my father believed in a ten percent tithe. That is off the gross not the net. When the basket came around the next morning it was expected that I would put in one of my dimes. We belonged to a church that preached tithing, but did not make it mandatory for membership or good standing, and I do not think that my dad checked up on us to see if we had put our tenth in, but he didn't need to; he set us the example, and trusted us to follow his lead. He was a good leader.

When I was twelve I became apostate. I did not, of course, tell my parents this. And in unspoken protest I withheld from the church the tithe of my considerable babysitting revenues. I decided instead to send my riches to a group that was saving baby harp seals in Nova Scotia. It never occurred to me to stop tithing just because I happened to be apostate. When I told my dad about this – the harp seals, not the apostasy - he was concerned, but asked only, "Is that what you think God would have you do?" I told him that I thought that Jesus really loved the baby harp seals, and that yes, it was what I felt led to do. He accepted my decision.

I have been a religious and philanthropic donor for as long as I can remember. I believe in it. I believe it is good for the giver and good for the world. I believe in giving locally, nationally, and internationally.

I support my local church. (My apostasy did not last into my twenties.) This is where the ancient practice of tithing comes in. If you have ten families, and everybody gives ten percent off the gross, then the rabbi eats as well as the average member. This has worked for millennia, no reason to challenge it now. I happen to believe that for all their problems religious organizations have done more good than harm. If you sit in a pew you should support the work of that group or find another pew you can support. Hopefully they are doing more than dusting pews.

I believe in doing some giving in secret. After my father left this planet to pursue other interests, I discovered that he was giving regularly to many organizations, some of them I knew about, some I did not. There was a group on the north side of Chicago that helps male prostitutes; my dad was a regular and generous supporter of their work. I got a phone call from their director when I sent a last check and a note to them. He choked up on the phone talking to me, telling me about the notes of encouragement that my dad would send with his checks. He said to me "I can find other money, but where am I going to find those good words?" Yeah, me too.

I believe in doing some giving spontaneously. Mostly I like to know where my money is going. I like to see annual reports and I like to see low overhead costs. I like accountability. But sometimes, the Spirit just says "Here, now" and I try and respond. I like to help the person in the grocery line in front of me when they cannot find that last buck they are looking for in the bottom of their purse. Nobody ever has to send an item back, if I am standing in the line behind them. Freaks people out – but it's a lot of fun.

However, I have heard a lot of lousy preaching about giving in my life. A lot of shameless hooey. Let me debunk a bit of it.

Giving to the church is **not** the same as giving to God. This silly notion gets put out there all the time. I heard Saint Bono say once, "My God does not need your cash!" It is just so obviously true. God owns it all. Did before you came along and will after you are long gone. Because it tickles God's cosmic fancy the Divine lets us push stuff around, but don't kid yourself, God is not a beggar. People who tell you that giving to them or their organization is the same as giving to God have ego, or possibly blasphemy, issues going on. Shame on them.

From which follows the corollary. Giving does not make you acceptable to God. God finds you acceptable. Face it, God's crazy about you – indulgent as all get out. This does not mean that God does not have issues with some of the stuff that you are doing, but you can't fix that by writing a check.

Giving is not a get rich formula. Giving to that which purports to be or even is God's work does not force God to give to you. It doesn't sway the Divine opinion of you in a way that makes God want to bless you. There is no magic here except this. When you give away some of your stuff, you are freed from the slavery to stuff. You place your bet on the kindness of the universe. You trust. And that changes you and frees you from the terrible lie that says there is not enough to go around, and then you find that you have plenty. And you feel a lot richer. People who are not fearful and mistrustful are more productive.

Here are some things I have found to be true about giving.

It does not matter how much you have or how much you give. If you have ten dimes, you can part with one. It is good for you to part with one. It is good to develop the Spiritual Discipline of Generosity. It is good to start when you are young. It is good to start with your first job. It is good to revisit your giving when you have a change in fortunes. It is fun to split a windfall. It is especially important to give when you don't feel like it, when it seems risky. It changes you, and you change your world.

My dad was never a wealthy man. He did not have a professional job or a college degree. We rented our home for most of my childhood. But he left his children a nice little bit, and when I took over his books at the very end, I discovered that he was giving 40% of his retirement income away. And that was off the gross, not the net.

Gratitude

So there I was ...

getting my clock cleaned weekly.

I was training to be a counselor. I was in my last term. I had 18 months of clinical practicum in my backpack. End of tunnel in sight – didn't expect that light to be an oncoming train.

I had a new supervisor and she did not appreciate me. I don't think that there was anything about me that she liked. And her disdain of all things Peggy Parsons was apparent in the first session. Our meetings focused on listening to, and critiquing, tapes of my counseling sessions – my clients signed up for this by getting a cheap student driver counselor. From the get-go it was apparent that she thought I could do nothing right. I remember her criticizing the tonal pitch of one of the sounds that counselors make to show empathetic listening. She didn't like it when I spoke, she didn't like it when I was silent. Realizing, of course, that a good supervisor would never give **only** criticism, she occasionally faintly praised ridiculously small things; as in "Well, Peggy at least you called your client by her proper name – that was adequate."

I never did figure out if there was anything I did to precipitate her treatment of me, but I do know the moment that I sealed the deal.

After weeks of tearing apart my work, we ended a meeting and I looked up at her shelf of books by feminist theologians and psychologists and said "Gee, you know, I would have thought that feminist supervision would have been a little more nurturing than this."

It wasn't a clever thing to say. After that she called the school I was to graduate from, and the clinic where I was doing my practicum and tried to get me held-back and fired. It's pretty rare to get held back a grade in graduate school, but she tried.

At that point, I was starting to wonder if, despite lots of evidence to the contrary, I really sucked at counseling. And if I did not, how I was going to get through the last couple of months of this ordeal.

I hired an independent person, another clinical supervisor, to give me some perspective. He listened to my tapes and told me that I was doing fine. I asked him for advice on surviving an upcoming exit interview, when my supervisor would meet with me and the director of the clinic where I was working. The one I was hoping would hire me after my graduation. I was certain that she was going to try and make sure that I did not get that job.

His advice; "Thank her."

"For what? – abusing me?"

"Yes, call it diligence and thank her for it. Make a list of everything you could possibly think of, and thank her for it. Thank her for providing you with a chair to sit in, thank her for agreeing to see you, thank her for her attention to detail. Start with that list – take up as much time as possible and then when she gets her say, argue with nothing and thank her again, in detail. Gratitude is your only option, any other response will look like defense or offense and they will both fail. But Peggy – you have to thank her sincerely, you can't sound facetious when you do it."

I didn't like his advice, but I took it. It was nasty hard to do, but I did it.

The look on her face was pretty precious, but the bottom line was that I graduated, got the job, and that woman has become an unnamed footnote in my story.

That was my first awareness of Gratitude as a spiritual discipline. I am grateful to her for that. Really.

My mom taught me to say thank-you – but that was usually for things that were good and that I liked. She gave me a way to express my natural gratitude. The discipline of being grateful when things are going to hell in a hand basket came harder and later.

But I have come to believe that it is a foundational spiritual discipline. It is the discipline that frees you to learn all the others. It completely circumvents resentment. It takes anger and divides it into that which requires action and that which can be released. Eliminating resentment and reducing anger allows you much more time for attendance. It makes failure bearable. It sweetens everything that is already sweet. If

I start and end my day with gratitude, nothing that happens in between has the power to ruin tomorrow.

A couple of years back I received a second-hand instruction from a Benedictine nun. It was shared with me by a friend, and it dropped immediately into that hole in my soul that is truth-shaped. She said, "Pray this prayer daily: Thank-you for everything – I have no complaint.'"

I have tried to do this, not just daily but hourly and moment-by-moment. It is not easy. Some things, like interruptions and thwartings, do not fall easily into the gratitude basket. I wrestled for a while with thanking God for things that I did not really believe that God was sending me. I do not believe it is God's explicit intention for me to be sick or stupid or in harm's way. But then I came to believe that these things were part of the global package and that for all its faults I choose to believe that the package is good.

Most of my problems are the consequences of my own foolish actions. I realized that having painful consequences for stupidity was indeed a gift from God, how else was I going to know when to change?

A smaller percentage of the things I hate are the consequences of other people's stupid actions. But I have learned to thank God for this because it gives me a chance to be perfected in my own reactions, and to step up to the plate for things like justice and peace.

The smallest percentage of my grief is in response to things that are not in human control, like death and sickness. This **is** God's deal – it is part of the set-up. I do not like it very often. But I have come to accept even these things, and to trust God in them.

The hardest part of this prayer is the choosing not to complain bit. For years I have used God as my unedited sounding board. If I have to yell at somebody, why not God? I mean God's a tough mother and can take it, right? God has always seemed patient about this, and after I rant a bit, I always feel better and settle into a better place. So to give up complaints seemed to be giving up one of my favorite coping mechanisms. It also seems at odds with justice. There is a lot of bad stuff going down on this planet; don't we need to make an issue of certain things? Shouldn't we complain?

What I have discovered is that forsaking complaint and moving into gratitude has zero affect on the truth, in fact, it makes truth clearer, and you can move straight to action.

"Dear God, thanks for this mess – I have no complaint – please get my back as I step into the middle of it."

Sometimes I need to do something. Sometimes I need to be something. I have found that gratitude is the fast track to the place where God needs me most, and where I most need God.

Release

So there I was ...

getting on a plane. Returning home, but leaving a huge chunk of my heart behind. I had just dropped my firstborn child off at college, half-way across the country, and every bit of 18 years of mommy conditioning told me I was being bad – very bad.

You do not dump your children off among strangers, hoping that they will figure out how to live in a foreign environment. You do not abdicate your responsibility for keeping the worst of the world at bay while they learn and grow. You do not suddenly cease your constant, if often unwelcome, teaching commentary on their life.

You do not just walk away. You just don't.

Except that we all do – eventually. At least every successful parent, does, eventually, just walk away. It didn't help that this was an extremely competent child, and that my mothering had mostly been consultative for the last year or two. The problem with competent children is that they often think that they can do all sorts of grown-up things – whether they can or not.

And it really didn't help that when I got home the family dog "yelled" at me for weeks. He would go into her room, bark, and then come in to me and bark at me.

"Stupid woman! You've lost your puppy!"

"I know, Alex, I know."

When his Lassie imitation failed, he fell into a depression that lasted until Christmas.

The girl, of course, was fine. I, however, was just starting my work in the Spiritual Discipline of Release. Some of the spiritual disciplines are optional; elective courses for the spiritually motivated and inquisitive, others are mandatory. Release is one of the mandatory ones, a core requisite. You can do it badly or you can master it, but you are going to take this class.

If you are lucky enough to live so long, you will release your parents, your children, and your lovers. You will eventually release your strength and whatever mental superiority you ever had. The more you are blessed, the more you will release, until the day comes when you release your very life. It may be ripped from your clinging grasp, or it may float away like the fall leaves, but you will let go of it. Fortunately Life, in its kindness, offers you many opportunities for practice before that day.

I have learned a few things that help. I have learned to breathe and relax my body on command, especially under stress. I have learned to pray. I have learned to trust God to be God and to run the universe, with or without me. I have learned how to discern if something is my problem or somebody else's problem, and I don't usually try and fix other people's problems. I have learned that control is an illusion, and that when I cease trying to control, my influence actually increases. I have learned to trust people, most of the time they do an adequate job with decent intent. All of these things help me let go.

Which is good because I am about to take a mid-term exam. I am about to walk away from my life for a couple of months.

This is a thing that competent, professional, middle-class American women rarely do. Like most of my age mates, I spin plates, and I spin with the best of them, I do. I lose a saucer every now and then, but no major losses. I have hearth and home, two part-time professions, and a handful of odd gigs on the side. Plus a dangerous hobby or two. And being me, I take a leadership role in most parts of my life. Much easier to lead than to follow, less frustration, usually turns out pretty well, my kudos cabinet is well stocked.

But there are some things that are so focus-consuming that you have to lay everything else down to have a chance of doing them right. I am about to go to an unstable, dangerous, alien part of the world, to do complicated assessment and training. It is a one plate, one pole spin.

So I have to let go of everything else for a bit. My counseling clients will have to take care of themselves or find other help. My fledgling church is going to fly without me. My family will run the house without my help. My second daughter will pack away the 120-year-old Christmas ornaments that I never let anyone else touch. The motorcycles will sit cold with batteries draining and oil sludging. The plants in my late father's greenhouse will pray for mild weather. And the

101 unforeseen mini-crises that are bound to occur during my absence will be handled or not by someone who is not me.

That same first daughter that I abandoned to her college life had a favorite Sesame Street bit when she was tiny. It was a musical number where Ernie wanted to play the saxophone but was having problems because it took two hands to play and one of his hands was occupied by holding his beloved rubber ducky. A conundrum. A series of famous cameo singers sang this advice to the orange everytoddler. "You gotta put down the ducky, yes, put down the ducky; you gotta put down the ducky if you wanna play the saxophone."

So watch me, I'm gonna take a deep breath, say a prayer, renounce control, and put down my beloved ducky of a life, and blow.

This column was written at the end of December 2006, immediately before I left for my second trip to Central Africa.

Retreat

So there I was ...

in the convent chapel. Listening to the Sisters of the Queen of Angels Monastery singing the evening praise. Tonight I was just listening. This is hard to do because the sisters are so hospitable that if you do not take a book of prayer out of the rack, they will assume that you don't know where they are and will get you one. If you have a book and do not open it, they will assume that you cannot find the right page and they will try and help you. As a Quaker, a severely unliturgical heathen, I do have trouble with the book. Sometimes, the seasons, the days, the songs, Psalms and Magnificats, get a little overwhelming. I do ok with the "Our Father," I have even picked up the "Hail Mary" although they don't seem to use that one so much in group worship. (I once said a full Novena, just to see if I could do it, and to see how it felt.) But sometimes I just like to close my eyes and listen. The sisters read a piece of the Book of Psalms out loud every day. The service has a brief reading from somewhere in the New Testament, but a big chunk of King David's lyrics daily. I wonder what he thinks of their rendition. I wonder if he wishes he was getting residuals – well, maybe he is.

There is something eerie about the voices of a few dozen gentle, kind, often elderly women, intoning the imprecatory Psalms. They put very little emotion into the words. David used many of his words to curse his enemies; swords in their hearts, destruction, wrath, revenge. The sisters give voice to these sentiments rather unsentimentally. I have never seen them flinch at even the most embarrassing parts – smashing the heads of the enemies' babies on rocks, etc. To their credit they to do not seem very inflated when they read David's words making the tenuous case for his own righteousness, either. They just speak these words out into the air, a display of the best and worst of the human condition, as if to say, "Hey, God, look at us – this is what we are – what are you going to do with us?"

Due to a trip to Africa, an illness, and a few other things, I had not been out to the monastery for six months. This had been the longest lapse in ten years of mostly monthly visits. I try and get out for a 24-hour retreat. I spend an hour or two with a Benedictine spiritual director, trying to take an honest look at my own spiritual condition and whatever notion God is attempting to squeeze into my feeble heart, brain and soul at any given time. Then I spend the rest of the time resting, or praying, or doing anything except my normal work and worry. It is good for me.

They don't like to let me work, although there is work to do out there--they all work as part of the Benedictine Rule. My spiritual director thinks that I am rather bad at Sabbath, and she is right, so I rest. She also doesn't ask me to keep silence as often as some. She thinks that as a Quaker I am probably good at this – which is not quite so true. But some of the sisters enjoy my dinner table tales of modest adventure, so I serve in my own way.

This trip out, after such a break, I was itchy. The American allergy to stillness and disconnect had me all but in hives. No iPod, no computer, no phone, no TV.

No to-do lists, no calendar, no demands on my time or attention. It is exactly what I wanted and needed and it about drove me crazy. What happened next was predictable. I crashed. Right after dinner I laid down on my bed for a minute, fell asleep, in my clothes, on top of the bedcovers, and I slept like that for fourteen hours. I was not sleep deprived, I am a good sleeper but my brain just couldn't stay conscious and do nothing. It was a shock to my system. My dreams were vivid and many, but confused and mildly disturbing. I woke up, had coffee and did some praying and writing. Then with my spiritual director's blessing, I took off a couple of hours early. I got back on my motorcycle and tripled the miles between the Monastery and home. The sisters like it when I bring the bike. They get a kick out of seeing it parked in front of their home, makes people wonder, I guess.

I left so much better than I came. It is kind of a Roto-Rooter for my soul. Sometimes I fly out there desperate for the break. Sometime I have to pull myself away and make myself go. It is a discipline. The Spiritual Discipline of Retreat. I have found that no matter how good I get at listening to God's Spirit in everyday life, that I regularly need to completely disconnect in order to reboot my hard drive. Stuff just runs better.

I recommend disengagement. You cannot spiritually advance without some kind of regular retreat. It may seem counter-intuitive, but it is true. It can take many forms, and you don't need the vocational religious, fun though they are. But you need it. Ask your soul.

Supplication

So there I was ...

trying to talk to Annabelle. I had known Annabelle for about fifteen minutes. It was my first day, on my first visit out of the USA, to the least developed country in Africa, Burundi. Annabelle was to be my household helper. I knew this because I was dropped off to an empty house and introduced to her.

My host knew that I had no Kirundi, Annabelle's first language, and he believed that she had none of mine. I was trying to learn Kiswahili, and though my helper had not had much school, she had plenty of Kiswahili, so my host commanded her to speak nothing else to me. Then he left.

I was to run my own household. Annabelle had no clue what I wanted, but understood the basics of what I needed. I needed to know when she would be coming, what services she would provide and we needed to negotiate her pay. Our attempts to communicate in Kiswahili lasted about fifteen minutes until we were both good and frustrated, and fell into our native tongues, and a bit of prayer. We discovered that we both had some French vocabulary and that Annabelle had a lot more English than she advertised. We started communicating in a badly mixed mess of four languages.

Annabelle's best sentence was:

"Give money moi." She said it with authority - almost a demanding tone.

I had "Kwa nini?" (Why? in Kiswahili.)

"Chakula, market" she said. (Food – Market)

OK, money to go to the market to buy food.

We worked on the currency and she left me.

After she left, I felt flustered. She seemed awfully bossy. I wondered if we were going to get along. It was only later that I found out an important fact. Kirundi has no word for "please," so Annabelle had no concept of "please," no way to ask nicely, no word to indicate supplication. She had the simple imperative, and nothing else. I started to think about a society with no verbal way to implore. The educated classes had picked up the French "S'il vou plait", if you please, but Annabelle did not observe the French niceties.

At that point, I needed Annabelle a lot more than she needed me. She did need a job. She was twenty-one years old and functionally an orphan taking care of seven younger siblings. She lived in the ghetto of Kamenge, and at that time, they were being chased out of their house at gunpoint three or four times a month. She was resilient, and resourceful, but a little cash was going to help.

I was also in need. I had no idea what I was doing. I had no way to feed myself. I didn't know what water was safe. Some of the insects in my house were harmless and a few turned out to be deadly. I didn't know one from the other. I didn't know how to get a taxi. I didn't know if it was safe to walk anywhere. I didn't know what to do when the electricity company came around and threatened to turn me off unless I paid them off. Annabelle was my key.

I was relieved to see her arrive the next morning with coffee, pineapple, and bread. I knew I needed her help and I knew I needed to learn to communicate with her. So I started learning, and by example teaching, the art and Spiritual Discipline of Supplication.

"Annabelle, please, s'il vou plait, tell me..." and we started around the house naming things. After things, we started working on behaviors and then higher concepts. She asked me questions. We still mixed four languages.

You cannot know how important supplication is until you recognize your need. I think everybody should be dropped on the equivalent of another planet once or twice to make this real. Another way to learn this is to develop a nice raging addiction and let it mess up your life. Then you get to do the First Step that every recovering alcoholic knows so well; "I came to realize that my life was unmanageable." Recognizing that you cannot make it on your own is a foundation for spiritual growth.

Americans are just so blessedly arrogant about this. We think we can manage anything: our lives, our country, your country. And it is just so obvious to everyone else that we are not so good at it. Spiritually, a lot of people have to hit bottom before they recognize that they have a need for a God. There are a lot more atheists in the middle and upper classes than among the poor. The poor and the sick will tell you that they know they need help.

After you recognize your need, you have to ask for help. Stop and ask for directions? How good are we at that? Not very. Let somebody else see our unmanageability, our need, and our weakness? Not our long suit – by a long shot. Welcome to Step Two – "I came to believe that a force greater than myself could help." You have to believe help is possible. You have to recognize it. You have to approach it – willing to be seen for what you are, and where you are.

Then you have to actually accept the help that comes your way. Step Three – "I made a decision to turn my will over to that power." This means that you ask, and you lay down your personal preferences and take the help that is given, not necessarily the help you asked for, or the help you thought you needed. They call this "Taking Life on Life's terms."

Then you "Let go and Let God."

You can sum this process up thusly:

"Oh Crap! Oh Look! Oh Help! OK."

This is actually an optional spiritual discipline. God will love you just as much if you never ask for help, or fail to recognize and accept the help that comes your way.

But ignoring this discipline may shorten your life exceedingly. And I guarantee it will impoverish your life tremendously.

I learned to ask Annabelle for many things. I didn't worry about looking like a Muzungu Ujinga – (Stupid white person) – because I was a Muzungu Ujinga. And she learned to take risks and ask me for things other than the necessary things. She learned to ask for what she really needed.

"Paygy" (That's how she said my name)

"Payge – pleeze - mange chakula moi?" (Peggy, please can I eat food?)

"Annabelle – vou mange today, Ijumaa?) (Have you eaten today, Friday?)

"Oya" (No)

"Ayya! Annabelle, vou mange chakula niumbani moi, ego?" (You eat food here at my house, yes?)

"Oya, never." (No, never)

I discovered that this girl came hungry to my house each morning and never touched more than a bite for the six to eight hours she was there, as she cooked three meals for me, because she believed that eating my food was forbidden. Thieves lose their jobs. I had no clue. I was sick.

"Annabelle! – Chakula Moi – Chakula Vou!" I said it with authority. (My food is your food)

The next day my host came in and found Annabelle sitting at my table having her breakfast with me, I had gotten up for the coffee pot and topped off both our cups, and offered him some. He looked surprised.

"Why are you serving Annabelle?"

"Why not?"

This story is from my first trip to Burundi in the fall of 2003

Surrender

So there I was ...

out in the back yard. I was twelve years old, it was springtime and I had just decided to become apostate.

One of the problems with this picture is that I was twelve and knew what apostasy was: willing, full knowing revolution against God and God's faith, a change of loyalty, defection. This was the choice of lucifer, the fallen one. Another problem was that it was precisely what I wanted.

At that age I looked a lot like Pippy Longstockings; skinny, straggly hair in two messy braids, tall for my age, pale, and weak. But I had left that Sunday evening class that was supposed to be my preparation for baptism and made a big decision. No thanks. I'll work for any team but yours.

My rebellion was supported by three pillars: God's people, God's teaching, and God.

Despite the fact that I had loving parents who walked their talk, they seemed to be an anomaly. The guy teaching my baptism class preached love and beat his kids. The big deal youth preacher down at Moody Bible Institute thought that the most important thing we could do as young Christians was to smash all our rock music. There were people telling me that I should simultaneously worry about college and the end of the world, which was going to happen any minute. These people seemed bad or nuts – take your pick.

Doctrine-wise I had picked up this: "Hey little girl, the best person who ever lived was brutally murdered and it was **your** fault." Nobody in our church ever debated whether to blame the Jews or the Romans, those nails were meant for your hands, and the guy with the hammer is just part of the plan. This was a bit heavy for a child.

And then there was my personal observation of God. He apparently stood by while the world was in a severe mess. His supposed cure on the cross did not seem to have had much effect. And I did not buy the notion that this was also our fault for not accepting Jesus as our Lord and Savior, because many of the people who did profess this acceptance were doing a lot of the bad stuff. I was twelve, but I understood racism, and the Christians who supported it. I understood and even approved of human free will, but I didn't like what God was doing with God's will. I didn't like how things were set up. I blamed God.

And so I stood there and looked at the sky and said this:

"I know you are there. I know you want me but I refuse you. I want nothing to do with you or your church. Go away and leave me alone. I will be just fine."

And then I went in and put on my PJ's, asked my mom for milk and cookies, read some Tolkien, and slept peacefully.

I may have been apostate, and courageous enough to tell God, but I wasn't stupid enough to tell my mom. So I started my life of closet apostasy and ironically, serious hypocrisy. I did decline baptism. I told my parents that I did not feel ready and that surely they wouldn't want me to be baptized until it felt right. They looked worried, but they agreed.

I eventually taught Sunday school, because it was easier than sitting in Sunday school. I was president of the youth group because somebody had to do it. I went to camp. I sang because it pleased my mother. I did precisely whatever pleased me the rest of the time. And I counted the days until my escape. I had some close scrapes running my own life, but I was making it. Sure I was scared, hiding a lot, faking a lot, but it was only temporary.

At eighteen, by a narrow margin, I achieved the velocity required to get out of the black hole suction of the nearby Christian College. I was accepted at a prestigious liberal arts school with no tests, texts, or lectures. It followed Mortimer Adler's regimen of the Great Books. I read Sophocles in Greek. Did science with Archimedes and contemplated Plato and then worked my way through history. Nobody told you what to think, they just asked questions and put up with know-it-all eighteen year olds like me. All this in the lovely city of Santa Fe, New Mexico – 1500 miles from home – paid for, of course, by my mother.   Freedom.

I drank beer. I rode horses. I got myself a guy. It was great. Until sophomore year.

They only had three questions at the School. You applied them to every text; what is the author saying?

Is it true? And if it is true, how does it change your life? I should have smelled a trap.

Because sophomore year we read the Bible. Cover to cover. And asking the questions were these two guys, our academic midwives and nursemaids. At one end of the seminar table was Michael Ossorgin, conceived in Russia, born in Paris just after the revolution, graduate of the Sorbonne. A Russian Orthodox Bishop – he chain-smoked and drank hard and glowed with holiness – this worried me a bit. At the other end of the table was Robert Sacks, Jew, slight of frame and fettered by cerebral palsy, he occasionally shouted, and often laughed and was a planetary expert on the Book of Genesis. He scared me a bit. They were absolutely nothing like anything I had ever seen before, only they were like everything I knew was true.

The Old Testament wasn't too bad. All those years of Sunday school helped me sound pretty smart – at least I thought so. Then we read the New Testament – in Greek - slowly. And there was that pesky Jesus - purported God. And those dirty questions. And the holy guys at the ends of the table.

In the beginning was the Word (reason, ratio, relationship, everything that ever made sense) and the Word was God. And this Word lights up everyone who ever came into the world. So often they do not recognize it. But if they do recognize it they become completely alive. (Paraphrase of John 1)

And I found that the truth wasn't in the book, or in other people – glowing or not – and it wasn't in the discussion or the dogma, or the reading, it was inside me, and I recognized it, and I began to live. I walked out of the seminar hall into the foothills of the Sangre de Cristo Mountains and I looked at the sky and I said:

"I know you are there/here. I know you want me/have me. I surrender."

And nothing changed and everything changed. But a conversation started that night that has never really stopped. I accepted Life on Life's terms. God is God. The deal is what it is. Huge pieces of the deal hurt. A lot of the people are unmitigated screw-ups, including me. But I am awake, alive, connected, real. I fake less. I am scared less.

And I have to surrender every day. It is not a one-time conversion sort of thing. I am asked to accept things as they are, not as I would have them be. It is the hard path to peace. It is the hardest of all the disciplines, and the most important.

This is what I know.

If that riptide tugging at your knees is God, dive for the undertow and drown.

Christ and the Lure of the Open Road

It is tempting to think of motorcycle riding as a spiritual discipline in itself. But I think of it more as a ground for practicing the disciplines. If spiritual disciplines exercise the soul then a motorcycle is a gym membership. It offers a consistent chance of gain. You can ride a bike and learn nothing from it, but why? It would be like going to the gym and never working out. There are lots of other grounds for spiritual learning. Motorcycles are, after all, optional and for some people not recommended, but it's my gym and I like it. Grab your lid and let's go.

Fresh Roads

So there I was ...

looking for fresh road. When I got my first motorcycle, one of the first things I did was go down to the State Department of Transportation and buy the big map of the county that I live in. It was several feet to a side and showed every road and alley within about 30 miles of my house. I started marking off each road as I covered it. Soon I had to purchase the maps for the five counties around my county and ride farther to get onto new pavement. Eventually my mega-map took up a whole wall of my house. After ten years and two bikes, I about had the State of Oregon covered; and Oregon is about 300 miles tall by 500 miles wide.

So around the turn of the century I was offered a preaching gig in Idaho and decided to take the opportunity to knock off some out of the way roads in the very far northeastern corner of the state.

Perhaps you do not understand why fresh road is so important. There is nothing that prevents the miracle in your back yard. There is nothing that slows down Sister Serendipity from meeting you at the corner grocery store if she is looking for you. The kingdom of Heaven is within you and can erupt at any time. However, the major inhibitor of that eruption is your own soul sleepiness. It is way too easy to get stuck on spiritual cruise control. Common intimacy encourages entropy.

The best way I know to break out of this is to find fresh road. I do it quite literally. Riding a road where I do not know what is around the next corner requires a level of awareness that makes me feel very lively. I have to pay attention. I cannot daydream. I know people who can find fresh road in a laboratory that they walk into every day for years. I know people who find fresh road on a blank piece of paper, or on the well-known strings of their favorite guitar.

Still, I like the wind. The unpredictability of the weather. So I was up in the country of Chief Joseph. His precious blue lake is still there. The Appaloosa descendents of his favorite ride live and eat this year's grass. His spirit and the spirit of his people flow down off those mountains towards the Snake River. That's where I was.

I reached the edge of the Snake after a long descent down the backside of the Wallowa Mountains on an unpaved road. I had been counting on a bridge over a dam on the map. The dam was there but it was no bridge. So like Joseph, I turned north towards Canada and several hundred miles out of my way. Unlike Joseph, my steed could not eat grass. But at least there was no cavalry at my back. My limits were the limits of a gas tank, not how far you could push the elders carrying the babies on their backs. I wasn't worried, because although the ranch houses were few and far between at that point, I knew that the ranch people kept a fill of gas cans and kindness, and the worst I could face was a walk or a wait. I talked to God and to Joseph and to the Appies in the fields.

And just after I had switched my fuel valve over to "reserve" meaning that I had less than a quart of petrol left, I saw a boy. About twelve. Walking.

"Hi Lady."

Blonde hair, freckles, big toothy smile, Huck Finn.

"Son, I need some gasoline and I need it pretty soon. How much trouble am I in?"

"Well, I wouldn't know about trouble, but if you take that next gravel road up there, you can cut through to the road that goes to the place where my dad drinks his coffee and Mrs. Wright, she has a pump in the back – you might have to ask."

"Thanks. Really, I mean it. Do you need a ride son?"

"No, ma'am, my Ma would switch my butt if I got caught takin' a ride with no helmet. Ma's pretty strict about the helmets. I don't have far to go."

"Sorry I don't have a spare, son. You take care."

"Bye Lady – oh, and the pie's really good – have the peach if she has any left."

The peach pie was fabulous. The shortcut got me there in less than ten miles. Mrs. Wright did indeed have a small reserve of gasoline. I described the boy to Mrs. Wright and the ranchers taking their coffee. I was hoping to speak a good word about him and his manners to someone who knew him. Maybe leave him a small reward – though I doubted any adult would convey a reward to a boy for just being neighborly – they would expect such.

Mrs. Wright and all the ranchers were of one mind that there was no boy of that description or even of that age, living on any ranch within 40 miles of that diner. They said they knew by name every child within that distance. I believed them.

I did another hundred miles of fresh road that day. Wide awake.

That road from the town of Joseph, Oregon down to the Snake is now paved, though I wouldn't recommend it except at high summer. You can visit the old Chief's grave up at Wallowa Lake; if you do, greet him for me.

The Samaritans

So there I was ...

at a truck stop on Interstate 40 in New Mexico. A 30-ish Hispanic trucker was sitting at the counter next to me. He kept stealing glances my way, presumably because of my black leathers and the motorcycle helmet next to my plate.

"My name's Hector, you out on the road?"

"Yep."

"All alone?"

"Mostly, I'm on my way home to Oregon from Texas."

(Hector looked impressed)

"I used to be a Disciple."

"Excuse me?"

"Back east, I rode with the Disciples"

(Ah, the motorcycle gang, the Disciples)

"I see."

"When I got to L.A., I rode with The Chosen Few."

"Well, it's nice to have friends."

"Sure is, you should find some; it's safer."

I told him that I sometimes rode with angels.

"No s**t."

"Not those Angels – the ones who work for God."

(Hector looked confused)

Over lunch, Hector regaled me with stories from his experiences as a one percenter.* Having immediately accepted me, he especially dwelt on stories about how the citizens (that would be you guys) misunderstand the bikers (that would be us). I especially remember one story he told me. He was out riding with about 50 or so of "The Few." They were rumbling along in formation out in the middle of nowhere when they came across an elderly couple in a big old Buick with a flat tire. Now you may not believe it, but bikers live under a strict code of conduct; it may not be your ethic, but an ethic it clearly is. They consider themselves to be good Samaritans, and children, the elderly, and other bikers often fall under protected status. So on that day "The Few" pulled over, en masse, to render assistance. For some unfathomable reason the elderly couple would not get out of the car. "The Few" did get them to pop the trunk where they found the spare tire. Unfortunately, the citizens did not have a jack.

"What kind of crazy people drive a car without a jack?" asked Hector.

"I do not know – citizens are unexplainable, my friend."

"This is true."

Being creative, a dozen or so of the boys gathered around the car and lifted the rear off the ground just enough for Hector and another man to change the tire. The moral of the story, according to Hector, is that some people don't know an angel when they see one.

"Ha! I made a joke – we weren't Angels – we were the Chosen Few."

"You are a funny man, Hector."

My biker friend was right, in a limited sort of a way; people are crazy. Some don't know a rescue when they see it; and some don't know what a neighbor looks like. Many see threats where there are none. But Hector's world was still divided into citizens and bikers. Categories of humans: Us versus Them. And that is just not right. The truth is, at times we're all old and weak and sitting in a cosmic Buick with a flat tire and no jack. And at other times we are the one with all the friends ready to gather around and lift. The key is to be attentive enough to see a need and pull over, or to be willing to see help arriving no matter what it looks like.

The one percent of motorcyclists who belong to "clubs" like the Disciples or Hell's Angels. Club members name themselves as "one percenters" with pride.

Running Towards Healing

So there I was ...

in need of healing, though I didn't really think of it that way at the time. I had recently been involved in a rather nasty sort of pastoral transition, the pastor in question being me. It involved, amongst other things, sexual harassment, conflict and deep disappointment. I had weathered the couple of months of clinical depression that followed and was just getting back on my feet when I took a short-term interim pastorate. Things were looking up, then four of my parishioners were murdered.

I had previously scheduled a personal retreat for just a few weeks later and I knew that I needed to take it, despite the circumstances. I had 96 hours set aside: Friday noon until Tuesday noon. I left Salem, Oregon, just after one p.m. on my motorcycle. The official plan was to go over to the coast and go a little ways south if weather permitted, or stay at a town named Florence if it rained. The weather did not look good at the start. My "Rule" was, no TV or newspapers, the Bible, but no biker bars.

I talk to God on these trips. I initiated my conversation with God with the very simple request of a little sunshine. It appeared, a small patch of blue always before me, but never over me, and I chased it all the way to the coast. Refueling at Florence, God spoke to me in the voice of a gas-station attendant, who said,

"You know, you can go a long ways chasing a little bit of blue sky."

I realized that this had been the condition of my soul all year; rained on, chasing, but never catching the bit of blue ahead of me. I turned south on highway 101 and rode faster. I realized that I was running when I hit the California border before dark, three hundred miles from home. I'm not sure what I was running to, or running from, but I was definitely running. I slept with the sound of the ocean in my ears and these words in my head:

"Wherever you run, I AM with you."

I spent Saturday buzzing through the Redwoods and down Highway One -- even smaller and closer to the Pacific Ocean. A guardian angel on a BMW bike pulled me over to warn me of an oil spill on the road ahead that surely would have taken me down, and I had lunch with two very old gay men on a Harley and a Moto Guzzi who wanted me to go with them to Baja. It was tempting, but my conversation with them caused me to explain to them and to myself why my commitments back in Oregon really did matter to me. Later, God and I had a nice light conversation about God's favorite color, and I was forced to take a very tiring detour over a mountain. I ended a ten-hour riding day in Bodega Bay talking to a prophetic waiter. I had gotten a notion in my head about visiting a certain church I had once heard about and asked the waiter for directions. He was surprised at the street names I gave him and asked why I wanted to go into that part of the "Tenderloin" district of San Francisco. I said I was going to church and he said,

"Ah, you are going to Glide Church. You are going to be OK."

Sunday morning I got up early and made the Golden Gate Bridge by 9 a.m. I made the 10 a.m. service at Glide United Methodist Church. I had heard a rumor about this place but I was in no way prepared for what I found. It was surreal; on my left was a prostitute who told me that she always "Stays ups for church – it's the only thing that gets me through." On my right was a guy in drag, I think, and the people in the pew in front of me were from France. They let the house band loose, and the stained glass shook. I am normally a strong introvert who dislikes and distrusts "enthusiasm" in worship. But that morning I bumped into the very real presence of a Holy, Righteous, and Rockin' God, and I clapped, and I danced, and I sang, and I cried, and somewhere during a song called "Restore my Joy," it was. I was healed, I carried no more wounds, my biochemistry was the same, my emotions were the same, but I was whole rather than damaged. I don't have any other words for it. After the service the prostitute said to me "You came a long way to get this didn't you?" I said "About 700 miles", she laughed and said, "Looks like longer than that, but it was worth it, wasn't it?" It was.

The ride home was a lark; I played a familiar game with my cosmic travel agent. Here is a true thing -- if you play with God, God plays right back. Sometimes on the road I play a challenge game where I name what conditions I wish to sleep under and see if God can produce them. OK, it's a silly game, but it is fun. That afternoon I requested a place to sleep in the trees with some Mexican food – a modest request. Within an hour I was registered in a little motel and restaurant on a wooded hill run by a very nice Mexican family. The only drawback was when I discovered that the room next to mine was "Sealed by the order of the Coroner." It seems someone had "checked out" rather permanently the night before. I stayed, and in a perusal of scripture that night, found what I took to be a new "life verse."

"Pray for me, and if I perish, I perish."
(Esther 4:16)

I do love God's sense of humor! Many miles north the next day, my joy still intact, knowing I would only make it to Grants Pass, a small redneck kind of town in southern Oregon, I made my request as ridiculous as I could. I wanted to sleep by a river, find a one-hour photo shop that was open after eight, and have New York cheesecake and cognac for a bedtime snack. At nine, photos in hand, cheesecake and cognac on a patio next to the river, I was left to wonder at the theologically ludicrous notion that the creator of the universe was spoiling me in a rather personal manner.

Tuesday noon I walked into my home, met my husband who asked if I had a good time. I acknowledged I had. He asked if I had gotten farther than Florence, and I handed him my pictures.

"Peggy, that's the Golden Gate Bridge."

"Yes"

"Peggy, that's you."

"Yes, it is."

"Peggy, that's in California!"

"Yes, it did seem a little weird; very like California."

"Peggy, what were you doing in San Francisco?"

"Getting healed, I think. Yes, getting healed."

Providence, Nevada

So there I was ...

in the middle of nowhere Nevada.

I was riding my Kawasaki Vulcan from Salem, Oregon to San Antonio, Texas, to preach at a women's clergy conference. It was April 1998, and I was about a third of the way there when my first major adventure occurred.

There is a whole lot of nothing out on Nevada State Route 95. It's about 300 miles long, from east of Reno to Las Vegas. It runs between several Air Force testing grounds and the California border, with Death Valley just on the other side. The scenery is remarkable, if you like stark and barren.

There are about three towns out there, two just big enough to have a gas station. At one station I actually had to crank the pump manually. The longest stretch of road was about 120 miles of serious nothing. At about 4 p.m. I was about half way across this stretch when my bike, Rosie, short for Rocinante, choked. She was at full throttle, then just a hint of warning, in the form of an acceleration loss, then dead, nothing. I coasted to a stop. She re-started, but sputtered and died again almost immediately.

I got out my cell phone to test my emergency system. I had a service called Mo Tow, if you break down any-where in the continental US and call them, they will come get you. I wasn't ready to call them for a ride yet, but I wanted to know that they were there. This is when

I learned a fundamental lesson about cell phones. They don't work without a cell tower. I was deep in the middle of "no service" land. If the Air Force was out there listening in Area 51, they weren't answering. Rats.

I started contemplating what I was going to do. It was too far to walk. I could not imagine abandoning my bike and gear and hitching a ride into Vegas. However, waiting all night in the desert cold for a state trooper, who probably wouldn't come, didn't seem like a good idea either. There were no ranches out here, and I hadn't seen another vehicle ahead or behind me for at least 30 miles.

I took out my spare two quart gas can and put it in the tank; pure superstition, as she had half a tank in her, but it seemed to cheer her up a bit. She started and stayed started. It was two hours until dark and I had 150 miles to go until I hit anything like civilization, even what passes for civilization in Nevada. We took off, but at full open throttle, the best she could give me was 25 mph. It was going to be a long cold ride and that if I was lucky. I started up a long hill, just waiting for her to stop again.

I started to pray, and I prayed hard. The road was rising precipitously, Rosie fighting like the "Little Engine that Could" to get us up. Then I topped the ridge and looked out over a huge caldera; a natural basin at least fifty miles wide, ringed by mountains. The sun was getting pretty close to the western slopes. Then, "Lo and Behold", as they say, out in the middle of the valley, I noticed a bunch of people and cars, tiny, like ants out on the plain, but clearly people and vehicles. I started down the slope. As I got closer, I saw that there were motorcycles! Dirt bikes out in the middle of the desert, racing in circles.

Rosie sputtered again and I started to coast. I could see the nearest group of vehicles. Sitting there by the side of the road, like a mirage, was a semi-trailer that read "Team Kawasaki - Race Team 1." I was thunderstruck, but I swear I heard the angels laughing. It started to sink in that there in the middle of the stinking desert, within a few miles of where my Kawasaki had trouble, were the best Kawasaki mechanics on the planet.

I rolled on in like a pit stop at Indy; well, more like a ghost into a pit stop in Hades because I arrived by gravity power, silent. Now, if I was surprised to see these guys, then I have to say that they were at least as surprised to see me. They were testing new bikes against team Honda and some others. Professionals only, no public invited. They had finished for the day, and they had won. They were celebrating, with enthusiasm, as they packed up their equipment. They were almost ready to roll off to the nearest hotel for the night.

I found myself surrounded by ten a dozen guys, most in their early twenties. Now, motorcycle mechanics run the same gamut of humanity as everyone else, some are bad characters but most are genuinely nice folks. As a lot, however, they are not particularly known for their couth or communication skills. I stopped Rosie in the dust and whipped off the helmet. I was grinning like an idiot at my good fortune, and they were grinning like idiots at the sight of me. Their first attempt at communication was to offer me the Jim Beam. I thanked them and declined. I tried to explain my predicament. After a little good-natured jesting they tried to listen to my description of the mechanical trouble. Then, just as I got to the part about the acceleration loss, they all, to a man, fell over laughing - I mean hysterics. I had absolutely no idea what I had said that was so funny. So I waited, and the most mature of the lot finally pulled himself together and said this:

"We know what's wrong with your bike."

"Great - Is it fixable?"

"Oh yeah, no problem."

"What's wrong?"

"Well, Lady, (Laughter), you got problems with your petcock." (Riotous laughter all around)

"I didn't actually know I had a pet cock," (Now they are on the ground again).

You may not think this is all that hilarious, but then, dear reader, you are not, thank Goodness, a drunken motorcycle mechanic.

Eventually I found out that there is a spring-loaded vacuum valve between the gas tank and the carbure-tors, called the petcock, which stops or starts the flow of gas. If this valve becomes jammed for any reason, gummed up, or vapor locked, no gas flows and you stop. The cure, oddly enough, was to open the gas tank and depressurize the tank. If this failed, you got off the bike, knelt by the side of the engine, unhooked the vacuum hose and sucked and blew the line clean.

The Kawasaki boys made sure that they instructed me in this practice and seemed to enjoy the spectacle. They checked out the rest of the bike, found me a plain old Coke somewhere, topped off Rosie's gas tank and assured me that I would get to Vegas. They sent me off with a big cheer. All in all they were nice fellows. Never say that our God does not have a sense of humor, or cannot use whomever for whatever purpose.

As I topped the next rise, I had the distinct feeling that if I turned around they would have all disappeared. It was a real "Twilight Zone" moment, if I had seen Rod Serling standing by the side of the road, I would not have been surprised. But then I bet those poor guys woke up the next morning with hangovers, and not sure if a woman on a Vulcan had really ridden in to camp yesterday afternoon.

But I have never, since that day, ever had an excuse to doubt God's providence. My God can, and does, meet my needs, in every circumstance, and with quality and humor.

The Joyful Art of Subversion

So there I was ...

sliding the motorcycle into a freeway rest stop – high summer, families out touring en masse. When riding, I am encased in a leather and Kevlar exoskeleton including full face, reflective helmet. It is not obvious who, or even what, I am. So when I whip the lid off, folks are often surprised to see a woman emerging from this cocoon. It's a little like sipping your Coke and finding out that it's a root beer – disconcerting expectations. After the startle, some people are interested. Little girls are especially curious. Their dads and brothers usually compliment me on the machine – girls want to know all about **me**. Countless times I have had this conversation in nearly identical form.

Little Girl: "Are you a lady?" (By which she means gender female?)

Me: "Yes, Indeed!"

LG: "Do you have a daddy?" (Are you married?)

M: "I do – he's at home."

LG: "He lets you ride a motorcycle?"

And then I lean down close, look LG right in the eyes, and whisper to her soul:

"I didn't ask – You don't have to ask!"

Ah, the sweet taste of subversion! LG rides off in the back of the minivan, eyes wide, looking back at me, thinking new thoughts.

Their moms ask similar questions, usually in the privacy of the ladies room, and they ask more obliquely.

"Does your husband ride with you?"

My answers to the mothers are also a little more oblique. I tell them that my husband doesn't care for motorcycles, but that we have an agreement that allows me all the safe fun I can handle. We leave alone the issue of what constitutes safe fun and who decides how much I can handle.

The mothers exhibit extreme surprise when I am off on a multi-state, multi-day ride. It is amazing to me how many adult women have never traveled farther than the mall unaccompanied by someone. They will travel in groups and gaggles, but rarely solo. Sometimes they get far enough into the questioning to ask where I am headed to that night. I often answer that I do not know, that I will stop when and wherever I get tired. I choose to trust God to supply the place. They usually stop asking questions at this point and back away. I become alien and a wee bit scary.

A Baptist minister once asked me how long Quakers have allowed women in the ministry. I answered, "Oh, 350 years or so – from the get-go."

And we didn't ask -- because you don't have to ask.

Making the Crooked Straight

"The voice of him who crieth in the wilderness, make straight in the desert a highway for our God. Every valley shall be exalted, and every mountain and hill shall be made low: and the crooked shall be made straight and the rough places plain."
(Isaiah 40:23-40)

So there I was ...

on a road between Highway 101 and Highway 1 in far northern California. A rainforest roller coaster of a road. Biker bliss.

I am not going to name the road because too many of you and your Winnebagos already know where it is. But it goes from the redwoods to the ocean, and it just might be the crookedest road in America – it is certainly my favorite motorcycle road. When they made this road through the prehistoric ferniness they banked those kinks and turns so precisely that a bike can whiz through there at speeds that cars can only dream of. Motorcycles chuckle at the suggested speed limits for those turns.

"Poor cagers – better slow down – Bye-bye!"

Because of the superb banking, centripetal forces glue the blessedly two-wheeled to the curves, allowing us to lean at angles that just shouldn't work. What appears to you citizens as a slow two-lane road is a four lane white-water rapid to us, and we use all those lanes. If you can see through the next curve, the whole curve is yours to slice. We do make the crooked straight.

We do like the rough places to be plain. Gravel is not our friend on that road or any other. We are balancing on about eight square inches of rubber, four up front and four behind. We need all the contact we can get.

I cannot ride that road without singing Handel's Messiah in the fabulous acoustics of my full-face helmet. Specifically the part where the prophet and lyricist Isaiah shouts out "Prepare a highway for our God."

Now it might seem at first listen that he is talking about the interstate through Nevada – flat, straight, smooth. But that is because you don't understand. God is the ultimate crotch rocket and humanity is stuck in the Winnebago. God is infinitely nimble, infinitely powerful, God has more lanes than you, God plays by completely different rules. And God will pass your 'bago on the right or the left like it was a concrete statue. And doesn't that just frost your cake? God so often behaves like a hooligan. Your messiest, most dangerous, serious switchback is God's pipeline – arrow straight, smooth and a kick in the pants.

And thus ends the metaphor because God does not wipe out.

The important thing to do in preparing the road for God, is to get out of God's way. Here is the message of Isaiah, of angels hanging over the heads of shepherds, of John the Baptist: something big is about to come this way! Clear the runway, turn on the lights, God is about to land a 747 in the middle of a hurricane! You are so going to wet your britches, but seriously, Fear Not!

I respectfully suggest that the next Ducati be named the Emmanuel.

How to Ride a Motorcycle with No Hands

So there I was ...

going about 85 on two wheels. I was a bit supra-legal, but it was on an empty, straight, flat piece of road on a clear, dry day in the middle of a county that has a population of about one person for every ten square miles – speed appropriate for the conditions.

My Kawasaki ZG1000 was big and new and it was not using half of the RPM's it had available. My back was not used to the forward lean of the sport bike seating configuration, so I would occasionally take one hand off the controls and twist my arm behind me to stretch out the kinks.

Taking your left hand off the controls of the bike has no effect. That hand is holding the clutch, and unless you are in the process of shifting, you can let go. The right hand is on the throttle, so unless your bike is equipped with some sort of cruise control, when you let go with the right hand, you start to slow down. But for the length of a stretch that is fine. Your right foot has a brake and your left foot has the gearshift. Control is diversified – a good idea whatever your endeavor.

It was during a round of this back stretching, including twisting in the seat and shifting my weight all around, that I came to realize a thing about my new bike. It is incredibly stable. It just hums along, rock solid, until you give it a clear and undeniable instruction

That is when the idea occurred to me. What happens if you take both hands off the bike at the same time? In grade school I used to ride my Schwinn "no hands" all the time. Would it be the same?

Impulse control has never been my deepest suit.

I covered both handles and then just loosened my grip incrementally until my hands were hovering but not touching the handlebars – no change except for the slow deceleration – nothing, nada. I gave it more gas and then let go again, this time putting my hands in my lap – like a train on rails. Gas again, and release, and then I pushed a bit with one knee and then the other. I could steer a bit this way, but mostly it just tore on like a bullet. Until I let the deceleration progress too far – instability started to creep back in at about 60. I gave it all four appendages again, exhilarated and thoughtful.

Stability increases with speed. This is true for motor-cycles. You are much more likely to drop your bike rolling it around a parking lot than you are at highway speeds. This is physics ala Brother Newton. It is called inertia – rule number one – moving things want to move, sitting things want to sit. On a bike, go fast and inertia is your friend speeding you along in a straight line. In a parking lot, inertia will gladly scratch up your paint, as your bike attempts to stay at rest. Of course, going too fast, inertia can cause personal aviation, especially if for any reason you forsake traction.

I am grateful for my riding experiences. I never fail to find spiritual application from the mindfulness that a bike requires of you. I have decided that I believe in the principle of Spiritual Inertia.

I have written about the need to sometimes slow down, way down, emotionally and spiritually in retreat. You have to fight the inertia of busyness to do it. But you reap rewards from it.

Yet, sometimes, positive inertia can be your friend.

When I am feeling emotionally and spiritually unstable, if rest doesn't fix it, then I probably need to give the engine some gas and get moving. Fight the inertia that would keep me stuck. I need to do the things in front of me: invest, engage, proceed. Sometimes I just need to trust the forward motion of my life to carry me across the occasional pothole to better road on the other side.

Probably might as well hang on, though.

Getting a Grip

So there I was ...

sliding across the Bridge of the Gods.

Spanning the mighty Columbia River a short ride east of Portland, Oregon, this bridge connects the states of Oregon and Washington at the approximate site where geologists and Native Americans agree there once was a stone land bridge that eventually fell into the river.

Falling into the river was also a concern of mine that day. I had never motorcycled this route before, so the sign stating that the bridge had a metal grate deck was a surprise to me, and the sign was not visible until it was too late to make any other choice but to cross.

Here is the problem with motorcycles and metal grating. The bike has about four square inches of each tire that contact the road at any time. That is eight square inches of grip altogether. Metal grating reduces those eight inches to a few tiny strips of metal. It is not enough grip. All traction is lost. It is like riding on ice. If all other things are equal and the grating is limited, then inertia is your friend, and if you just hang on, relax, and trust, the bike will continue forward without much deviation until you get solid pavement back. You do not dare steer, brake or accelerate. Brother Newton again.

All things were not equal on the Bridge of the Gods that day. I was traveling north to south and the winds coming up the Columbia Gorge from the west were about 30 miles per hour steady, with gusts exceeding that by a good bit. Without traction the winds were steadily pushing me to the left, towards the oncoming traffic. I had just enough warning to enter the grated section at the far right edge of a bridge that is 35 feet wide – 17.5 feet for me, 17.5 feet for the other guys. At that point it was a Hail Mary situation. Would my speed get me across the grate before the wind pushed me into the path of a semi?

That was when I made the mistake of looking down, past my feet, through the grate, and 150 feet down to the water. My head started to swim and I snapped my eyes back up to the road. An oncoming Winnebago was laying on its horn. As my tire touched the centerline, the grate ended and I had enough traction to correct my course. I coasted down to the tollbooth at the foot of this deathtrap. I was shaking badly enough as I tried to fumble into the pockets of my leathers to find the fifty cents required, that the toll taker shook her head and waved me on. I had the feeling she had seen rattled bikers before.

Spiritual lives can also lose traction. We can lose our connection with the ground. We can get all slip-slidey. Think about the places where the rubber meets the road in your life. They are not usually the most pleasant places. Friction is implied in traction. But those are the places that keep you grounded, that give you the option of relative control.

I find that if I surround myself only with people who agree with me, that I start to lose my moorings. I feel my connection to God in a very real way when I am around people who don't share my experience of God. This is spiritual traction.

I need a regular connection with people honest enough to let me know when my spiritual slip is showing or I have spinach in my teeth. We have all seen the hard public lessons of those who surround themselves with sycophants. Honest friends supply traction.

I lose traction when I get disconnected from the real physical needs of the least among us. I have learned that I cannot fix all the problems that I see. But I can do something, every day, every week, every month, to address those problems. Real, fulfilling work increases traction.

All of these conditions describe places where the road can fall below the minimum required grippiness. Sometimes the warning signs are there; sometimes we learn the hard way and mark our own mental maps for the danger.

We have to pay attention to the road because our culture has some prevailing winds: rabid individualism, materialism, affluenza, addiction to addictions. It does not matter how big my spiritual engine is, how strong my personal braking system is, if I am not grounded, the prevailing winds will push me out of my chosen lane, and that oncoming Winnebago will show up, horn blaring.

Stopping

So there I was ...

on the freeway, close enough to the speed limit. Sunny spring day. Singing a song with my angels in the fabulous acoustics of the full-face helmet. The wind was singing along too, because it was warm enough that I had the face screen cracked half an inch for temperature moderation. Then the universe required that I stop. Immediately.

The request came in the form of a bumblebee, which managed to defy the air stream flowing over my aerodynamic head and make a solid, eye-level hit at 70 miles an hour and yet live. Groggy but not stunned, it crawled into the only opening available for safe haven, my slightly open face shield. I felt it on my lower lip. I swallowed a yell and willed my mouth shut. I gave a mighty snort to try and expel it. It buzzed angrily like a throttle twist on a Japanese speed bike. I pushed my visor full open – but the air coming in glued the bug to my face. I turned my head. It crawled up from my lip and across my cheek, then up and over my ear and into my hair. There was more buzzing and thrashing up there as it unsuccessfully tried to escape.

At that point I pried my attention away from the bee and onto the road. I was in the middle lane of three; I needed to make a lane change and a prompt stop. I scanned ahead, behind, and to the side. I had lots of room. I signaled. I slowed, moved over, and slowed some more. I signaled, slowed and moved onto the shoulder. My back end fishtailed a little bit, when the bee made an especially angry protest and I reflexively stomped on my brakes, locking them for a second. I lightened up. I came to a swift but controlled stop on the gravel.

I used the kill switch on the engine and had the buckles off of my chinstrap in record time. Off with the helmet. Loose the long hair. Shake. The bee left. I had not been stung.

The bee lived by God's own miracle. I lived because of a cool head and good habits. I ride with the intent of always keeping a good stopping distance between me and whatever is in front, and if possible, a similar space off my stern. A good stopping distance is that space which allows for a graceful, safe deceleration. Speed increases the need for space. Poking along – not much required. Cruising at what I call "God Speed," I like the length of two semi-trailers. For cagers - you people in cars - the "two-second rule" applies. Use any non-moving object as the mark and count two full seconds from the time the car in front of you passes it until you pass the mark.

I like to have more space than that, before and behind. Even though motorcycles have a distinct advantage over cars in the acceleration/deceleration department, (this due to our smaller mass) I want as much space as I can have. Because life sometimes puts a bee in your bonnet.

Now, I know that those of you who drive in urban environments have a greater challenge with this. Other vehicles do not want you to have this space and will move into any space six inches larger than their cage. In California they will connect these spaces across three or four lanes and "surf." This increases your challenge, but the challenge to maintain the best possible safety bubble is still important.

And herein lies another spiritual lesson learned while riding. The spaces in your life are just as important as the objects. And you will need them at precisely the points where you will not have the time to pay attention to them. You have to build the habit of space into your life. Because you are going to have circumstances that stop you, suddenly, emotionally, physically, and spiritually. Some of them you may see coming and have time to reduce your speed and lengthen your space. Others will hit you with no warning at all. And you are going to stop; the only question is how gracefully.

The more I do, the more grace space I need. One way I increase my space is by investing in people, not things. That way when something happens, I know I can count on grace from people whom I have graced. They cut me slack, they lend me a hand, and they make room for me in many ways.

I build in the habit of space in my life by protecting my bubble of alone time, of quiet time, of nourishing time with God. Most months these times feel like luxuries. But occasionally they are life-savers.

The most important part of creating appropriate space around me is just attending. Watching to see if there is something sneaking up on me. Adjusting my pace according to the traffic of my life. Not letting people steal my space. This observation and adjustment process keeps me awake, keeps me alive.

One day all of us are going to get that final red light, that "pavement ends ahead" sign. It may come on suddenly, or we may see it coming for miles, but it will come. The end is not up to us, but how we do it is. We can go screeching into that end with our brakes locked and screaming, or we can execute a nice controlled stop. The way you have lived your life is going to determine how you die. I want to be able to pull over and hand the keys over with some dignity and grace.

Might as well practice stopping now.

A Way of Escape

So there I was ...

looking for a way through.

I was motorcycling down a major arterial in my neighborhood. It was a sunny, dry morning and traffic was light. Stopped at the next side street on my right was our local letter carrier. His name is Gerry. He is a friend of mine. I always smile when I see him in his postal truck. He is a good man and a good presence in our neighborhood. He knows me, and my bikes. As I came up to him, I smiled – I had my visor up. He was looking right at me. I thought we made eye contact. I nodded my head (can't always wave on a bike). Then, just as I approached the street, he pulled out – right in front of me – making a left turn onto the big street. I had one nanosecond to decide what to do before I hit the side of his truck.

When you are in motorcycle safety school (and no one should ride without this experience) they drum into your head that you must always be scanning the road ahead for potential dangers and potential solutions to those dangers.

The advantages of the bike over the cage are maneuverability and quicker acceleration/deceleration. We can go, stop, and turn faster than you can. This is a simple fact of physics; much less mass, nearly equal power. This saves our lives – a lot.

One of our major disadvantages is visibility. We are smaller and your brain is accustomed to notice cars and trucks, and often you just don't see us, even when you see us. This endangers our lives – a lot.

After alcohol and excess speed – both completely avoidable – the number one cause of motorcycle deaths is a car making a turn into your immediate path. This is unavoidable. But it is manageable. You make a mental discipline of presuming that you are either invisible, or if visible, that the vehicle ahead will attempt to intentionally kill you. Making this presumption, you plan your way of escape. There is always a way of escape, usually more than one. You ride your bike in a manner that makes escape possible at any time. Then you get to live.

On the day of my near postal collision, I had four choices; none of them really good.

1-Swerve left – in front of his path. He might stop at the last second and I could scoot in front of him. I rejected this, as it is folly to bank on his seeing me, when he clearly had not seen me to this point.

2- Swerve right – and try and go behind him as he continued his left turn. This might work if he moved quickly enough, but it presumed that he would not see me at the last second and hit his brakes. In my experience they almost always see you at some point and slamming on the brakes is always the natural response. I rejected this because it bet my safety on his response. I like to keep my safety in my own hands whenever possible.

3- Try and make the right hand turn. Move onto the street that he was leaving. This could work if I did not have too much speed going into the turn. It would require lots of lean for my cruiser-style bike. If I failed, I would go down into a slide, but that is preferable to hitting a large object directly. People survive slides. I was wearing good leathers.

4- Attempt the very fast emergency stop. If you are not going too fast this often works. But if you lock up your brakes you slide, often into the object you are trying to avoid. Going under a truck is not recommended.

There was not actually time to think through these options. These options had to be wired into my sinews and nerve endings.

I attempted a combo of three and four. He did see me at the last moment and he did slam on his brakes, coming to a stop, completely blocking the road in front of me. I turned to the right, leaned, and put the bike into a controlled sideways slide. I stood up, foot on my back brake and hand on the front brake. I was prepared to attempt to leave the bike if she went under the truck. I sacrificed a lot of good tire tread. And I stopped, facing to the right, parallel to the truck, smack dab at Gerry's driver side window. I stood the bike upright. I had managed not to soil myself.

Gerry looked down at me and said "Expletive, Peg, expletive I'm sorry. I did not expletive see you! Expletive!"

I looked up and said. "Expletive Gerry! Good thing I saw you! You almost expletive killed me! That would have sucked!"

Gerry: "No expletive!"

We were blocking traffic in two directions. He moved his truck across the street. I moved the bike to the side street. We both stayed put until we recovered. We did both recover.

This is yet another set of motorcycle truths that easily move into the spiritual realm. Don't travel so fast that you don't have time to deal with emergencies. Scan your horizon for trouble, but do it with a calm, relaxed, open attitude – fear and panic are not your friends. Always look for the way of escape – it is always there.

The Apostle Paul talks to the folks in Corinth about this. He says:

> *"There is not a situation that will test you that is not natural and common. God is faithful and fair. You will not be tested above your skill level. With the test there always comes a way of escape."*
> (1 Corinthians 10:13)

The word I have translated as test is often translated temptation, but test or trial is also a fair use of the Greek. So is assay, like checking the level of a precious metal. This passage is often preached narrowly as being about temptation to sin. And the "take away" is – You have no excuse for sin, there is always a way out. This is fair, but limited exegesis.

We do not learn without opportunities to test and use our skills. But we do not need to fear God as an assayer. God is not trying to catch us being bad; God is a fair educator who is on our side. Giving us skills, the opportunities to use them, and a way to survive and thrive during the learning process. God made us, and knows that we have "the right stuff." God wants to use that stuff to whatever level we will take it.

With God there is always a chance to retake the test. With motorcycles, inattention can take away the re-test.

So ride safe! Shiny side up, rubber side down!

Keep your eyes open and mind your escape route.

Quakers - Not Just For Breakfast Anymore

The Religious Society of Friends, or Quakers, have been around since the 1650s. It was an attempt, not to reform the Christian Church, but to replace it. We have not succeeded, but by most accounts we have added something significant to the conversation. The original idea was to go directly back to the feet of the rabbi Jesus Bar Joseph Nazarati and start with the Master's teaching, and then to let application of those teachings be made by the Spirit of the Present Christ without intermediary. We don't always succeed at that either. But many of us try. In 350 years, Quakerism has diversified significantly. Because of this diversity I can only testify to my own understanding of Quakerism.

If you would like to know more about Quakers, I recommend Quakerinfo.org

The Standard Jesus Stuff

So there I was ...

at a truck stop, stocking up on a warm breakfast to keep me going through a long day of motorcycle riding. My ride is a Kawasaki Vulcan 750 named Rocinante, or Rosie, or just "The Holy Kaw." When I am out on the road my mode of transport is obvious, even when she is parked outside because I am always wearing leathers and there is a full-face helmet on the counter next to me. I usually take a seat at the counter because the leathers don't bend so good, and it's a pain to get in and out of them.

I always mind my own business, but that never seems to prevent other people from minding my business with me. A big trucker plants himself next to me. The correlation between truckers and bikers is significantly high.

"Hey, pretty lady, where you riding to today?"

They never seem to be able to leave the solo female biker thing alone. But I take no offense. I give a brief itinerary. Weather is discussed -- I never discount weather info from a trucker.

"So, whatcha do when you aren't ridin'?"

"I'm a Quaker preacher."

This always stops them for a moment. Silence ensues, which is appropriate since Quakers often worship in silence. The next question is often,

"I thought you guys were all dead."

We are often confused with the Shakers – an 18th century sect that did not believe in procreation and hence mostly died out. Quakers have been around since 1652, have had women preachers all that time, and, for good or ill, we do have children.

"Nope, we're still going strong."

"And you ride motorcycles?"

Confusion with the Amish is next. Quakers have no conscience against technology per se.

"Yep, and cars and airplanes and everything."

"Hunh" I can see the confusion generalizing. I decide to volunteer a bit of information.

"And, we don't look like the Quaker Oats guy anymore."

"I can see that – but you **are** eating the oatmeal."

"Oh yes, we are **very** religious about the oatmeal."

Actually, Quakers have never produced, sold, or had any official connection with commercial oatmeal production. Those guys are trading off of our good name. I think we should get a discount, but we don't. However, sometimes I just can't resist messing with the heads of random truckers.

"So what are y'all about?"

"Oh, you know, the standard Jesus stuff -- being good to folks even when they aren't good to you, taking care of the poor, keeping it simple, telling it like it is."

"Hunh"

"OK, we don't really care so much about the oatmeal. Cream of Wheat is perfectly acceptable." (Caught by my own preaching once again.)

"You know, I always thought Jesus would make a good biker."

"Me too, buddy, me too."

The Big Deal of Little Words

So there I was ...

front row center for the first week of seminary - Beginning Greek class to be specific. I was all jacked up for this class because though I do not have any great giftedness for languages, I did have interest. I was one of those geeky little kids who tried to learn Elvish after my first reading of Tolkien. I had self-taught myself a little Latin. I went to a college where they made you read Sophocles in the original. Now, many years later with a much rustier brain, I was going back into the Greek to read the New Testament. I knew that Jesus himself probably did not speak in Greek to the disciples - most likely Aramaic, or Hebrew in Temple - but I was about to get a lot closer to his words than the King's English would ever allow. I was excited.

I noticed that many of my fellow students seemed equally stirred up. We were in the First Chapter of the Gospel of John.

"In the beginning was the Word, and the Word was with God, and the Word was God... and the Word became flesh and dwelt among us."

This is some of the most beautiful poetry ever written, and some of the simplest Greek in the New Testament. This is why our brilliant teacher had taken us there on the first day. She knew that she could get us through it and that we would feel like translators right off the mark. She wisely also let us bump right into the frustrations of translation. The bigger words were easy.

The verbs she gave to us on that day, but she let us struggle a bit with the little words, the prepositions, "in," "with" and "among." She explained to us that many of the words had multiple meanings and that the translator had to use wisdom, discernment, and context to decide which word to supply to the text.

This is when some of my fellow students started to get nervous. They also were there to get closer to the words of Jesus, but some were hoping to ease their frustration with the multiple English translations and find out what the "correct" answer was. They were searching for certainty, and the professor kept bogging them down in discernment. And they were discovering quickly that the little words could change the meaning in a big way. "*The Word became flesh and dwelt **among** us*" can also be translated "*The Word became flesh and dwelt **in** us.*" In fact, "*in*" is the more common translation of the Greek "*en*" than "*among*." The students saw the theo-logical conundrum of the choice almost immediately. They asked the teacher for the right answer. She told them why most translators chose "*among*" over "*in*", but allowed as how "*in*" was also a correct choice. Some of my fellow students started to breathe funny. They did not like the idea of two correct choices. They had not come to find a deeper level of mushy, they wanted solid. She gave them "context" and "translator's choice." Smoke started to come out of some of their ears. Some of them had spinners for eyes. Some of them started making plans right then and there to transfer to the Baptist seminary across town. I watched them for a minute with amusement, fundamentalists often amuse me. But then I got lost in the theological possibilities.

Prepositions of place count. Whether God is near you, or in you, matters - a lot. Since babyhood I had been told that Jesus was near me, knocking on the door of my heart, wanting to come in. John the Evangelist seemed to be implying in a big way, in many places, that God and Christ were already in me, in everybody, and had been since I came into the world and possibly before. That Jesus had planted the seed of Himself in me, in everyone, and was sitting there waiting for the right conditions to germinate.

This started a bout of thinking that continues in me to this day. You have to be in a kinda strong and grounded place to work on this puzzle. You have to be pretty comfy with paradox. The Apostle Paul talked about riddles wrapped in enigmas viewed in murky mirrors – yeah, that kind of clear.

Here is the problem. The Kingdom of Heaven is in me. It was in me in some form before I recognized it, and with my intention, called it to quickness. But it is also all around me; I can see it and observe it in my garden and in the stars. And is it also among us – in community with all its frustrations and foibles. I couldn't get more than a heartbeat away from the kingdom if I tried, it is that close.

And yet, Jesus said that He stands at the door and knocks, waiting, beyond some kind of barrier. The door is a metaphor for some kind of barrier. My fundamentalist childhood said that the barrier was my sin, that I was depraved. Fallen. That evil was inside me and that Goodness had to ask to come in. That has never set right with me.

I like all kinds of stories. In the theological metaphor that is "Buffy the Vampire Slayer," The Apostle Joss* sets things up where Vampires (evil) cannot walk into the home (heart) uninvited. Humans carry their glory and sin and possibility of redemption with them wherever they go. Goodness (God) is already in the house, it came in with you, and evil has to beg entry. For a professed non-believer, Joss is fairly Gnostic. Joss could be burned at the stake in certain inquisitions.

Me too. I am a Quaker.

When I face theological conundrums, I try and hold them as precious and deny none of it. I live with it until I wrestle a blessing out of it. But when I have to make a functional decision, my experience of God trumps dogma and exegesis. This I know to be true. When I first called out to Christ as a knowing adult, and sought His presence, He answered not from a place external to me, but from inside my soul. I work for the Kingdom, I fight the Lamb's War with the presumption that Christ is ahead of me working **in** everyone. All I have to do is find where He is working and assist.

I have met evil, but I have never experienced it as internal. It is always dissonant. Always wrong. Always against whom I was meant to be. Evil talks to me from outside. Christ talks to me from inside. I do have troubles sometimes with my listening, but I don't have a problem confusing the two.

This has made some startling differences in the way I do evangelism.

I cannot "bring anyone to Christ." He is already there. No one is "lost." He knows precisely where they are and what they need and He is on the job. I don't have to spend any prayer time, any worship time, inviting Him to come – we can just get on with it. I do not have to beg Him to hear my prayer. He cannot fail to hear it. Do you know how much time this saves?

So what can I do? I can preach the Good News. The Kingdom of Heaven is at hand. As close as your own palm print actually. I can fan the burning embers of desire for faith into crackling little flames. I can tell people the truth about who they really are and what they were put here to do. I can participate in the laboratory of sanctification that is spiritual community. I can walk the roads of my vicinity looking in the ditches for the wounded and dying. And sometimes I can stand out on the porch with the vampires and back them off a bit so that the people in the house can enjoy their redemption and do their work in peace.

And I have found that the paradoxes and conundrums become precious mysteries to explore when I have time, not problems that cause my hard drive to smoke.

It's a good deal.

Joss Whedon wrote and produced "Buffy the Vampire Slayer." It aired from 1997 – 2003. It is brilliant.

God Does Not Need Your Praise

So there I was...

sitting on a polished hardwood church pew. I couldn't have been very old because my patent leather Mary Jane's were swinging freely, well above the floor. We were all singing the Doxology, of course at that age I didn't know it was called the Doxology, it was just the song that came after they passed the pretty wooden plate with the red velvet liner. I had been singing this song since I was about two; of course I had been singing it by rote memory, syllable by syllable without understanding.

> Prays God Frum who mall bleh sings flow
> Prays Hih mall cree chairs hear bee low
> Prays hih ma buv yee hev in lee hose
> Prays Fa thur sun and hole ee Ghost
> Ah, MEN!

I had been singing this on call in my baby soprano to much applause. But as far as I was concerned, it might have as well been in Latin, or Martian.

And then on that one Sunday, about age five, something in my brain clicked and I realized the song was in English and that I understood the words.

> Praise God from whom all blessing flow!
> Praise Him all creatures here below!
> Praise Him above, ye heavenly hosts!
> Praise Father, Son, and Holy Ghost!
> Amen.

It was quite a little epiphany. And it was my first chance to actually do any praising, since it was my first understanding that any praising was going on. I dutifully reported to my mother that the song actually meant something.

But it started my little head a thinkin'. First, I had to work out my confusion about the trinity. I had a notion for God the Father, and Jesus was a regular figure on the Sunday school Flannelgraph board, but this Holy Ghost guy was confusing. Back then he was definitely billed as the Holy Ghost, not Holy Spirit, and this caused great confusion for me with Casper the Friendly Ghost. This was made worse by visiting the church of my Pentecostal cousins, because every time the Holy Ghost showed up, all the grownups started yelling and running around, which was precisely what happened in the cartoon.

Life can be confusing for children in religious families.

Then, after a while, I started to wonder about the whole idea of praising God.

I had a great mother. She believed in praising children for their good behavior and accomplishments more than punishing them for their wrongs and failings. I knew my mother loved me, and that she enjoyed her children, but even as a kid I understood that there was an ulterior motive in the praise. She was manipulating our behavior, and mostly it worked. It was a good system.

So I mean, really, did God need to be flattered, to have his good behavior reinforced? To prevent Divine temper tantrums? Did He need to be told how good He was? And weren't we God's children, so shouldn't He be praising us? To let us know when our deeds were approvable? Church music telling God how good He was began to be a problem for me. (When I was a kid, God was definitely a "He")

Things did not get better with the introduction of pop music into the church in the 60s and 70s. In a decade we went from preachers who tried to convince kids to smash their records of "the devil's music" to preachers in white-guy afro's trying to do Jesus pop/rock.

In most protestant churches, music wars resulted. In bigger churches, segregation of worship services by musical preference became common and continues to this day. Refugees from the Christian style wars started their own churches where they did not have to argue about it. They embraced the theory that cool, hip new music would bring people in the door and you could work on their belief systems later. This is still a popular theory. In many churches the balance of the worship service changed from an egalitarian mix of music, prayer, and preaching, to lots of praise music with a medicinal capsule of doctrine slipped in at some point. Of course most of the music was neither hip nor cool, it was third-rate treacle imitating the second-rate treacle of the popular genre.

Melodramatic, sexually frustrated, mostly drug de-prived teenagers, especially the girls, loved it because you could work yourself into a nice emotional state with a semi-orgasmic conversion experience at the end, all the while keeping it public and holy.

And we were told that this was precisely what God wanted. That God just eats this stuff up. That Heaven is pretty much going to be an eternal praise service with a kick-butt band. Well, at least we could hope the band would be better.

I watched this and wondered what kind of God this was, some cosmic, insecure Hollywood starlet who needed a multitudinous posse of sycophants to prop up the divine ego? I had better self-esteem than that, and I was 13.

After taking a long break from the whole thing, I came back to my faith, and back to Christian music through my hillbilly roots. Bluegrass and Southern harmony had a lot more meat, reality and integrity than the vast majority of "Contemporary Christian Music."

But as I became more involved in organized religion, I had to deal with the issue on an adult level. There was no doubt in my mind that scripture praises God and recommends praise as an activity. King David did it, Jesus did it, and Paul did it. Two thousand years of Christian history has included the practice. I really couldn't just blow it off. But I could never come to grips with a God who needed our praise, or who was moved by it.

Then one day while swinging my heels over the edge of another pew, I had another little epiphany. God doesn't need my praise. God isn't changed by my praise. I need to speak about the goodness of the world and the world's Creator because it detoxifies my soul. I hear constant messages about how this life stinks and how the world is going to hell in a hand basket and why I should be very afraid, and maybe despair, and none of it is true. I have to counter that poison with something. Gratitude and praise is that something.

When I sit in my Quaker meeting, we have no preacher and no band. We reach a nice balance. We sing a little, often positive affirmations of God's goodness – no shame, no guilt. We find the truest stuff that we can. Some of it is new, some of it is very old, some of it we have had to write. We try and avoid treacle. We detox ourselves and start to detox the space around us when we put the truth out there. We pray a little, and then we get real quiet and listen. No big Sunday emotional feast that leaves us hungry by mid-week. And no notion that God sits hungry, waiting for us to show up and offer a meal of flattery.

AH MEN

Call Me Irresponsible

So there I was ...

in a rural town in Southern Oregon doing domestic violence prevention work. Traveling preacher. Traveling feminist. Public Quaker. And the guy in the back was yelling at me.

We were having a series of educational meetings: warning signs of abusive personality, universal rights of women, how to get a restraining order. That sort of thing. At the time, the county we were in had the highest rate of domestic violence in the state.

The first evening a man came in and stood in the back. He was pretty sketchy looking. Not a big fan of the bath. Not a big fan of clean clothing. Apparently not a big fan of me and my material, because every time I said anything, he shouted at me. If I said "X" he yelled "Not X!" If I said "Y" he shouted, "Y is a lie!" and added a few cuss words. I could have had him removed. One of the local leaders asked me if I wanted them to shut him up or throw him out, and I said "No, leave him be, for once I am not preaching to the choir – this guy needs to be here."

So I just kept going. The next morning the guy came back, this time he took a seat and confined his comments to loud grumbling. He came back every session, until Sunday morning, when he came and sat in the front row. He had clearly washed his face – just his face, and maybe put on a clean shirt. I preached on the high opinion that God has of humanity, how we are loved, and that this love is extended to all, even the perpetrators of bad acts. Part way through my message, at the reading of some scripture passages about how God feels about us, this fellow suddenly caught my attention. He was shaking, silently; it looked like he was having an epileptic fit. Then there was noise, sobbing, and it was clear that the man was having some unaccustomed emotions. This time the elders did take him out, and I am told that he confessed to a long bad life and especially to a lot of spousal abuse. The elders paid a visit to his home, and provided assistance to the woman who lived there. The last time I saw the man, a couple of years after that morning, he was sitting on the floor of the meetinghouse, playing with the babies, clean, sober, and transformed.

This week they called Barack Obama irresponsible.* This, for saying that he would be willing to talk to our nation's enemies. Not compromise with our enemies, not make concessions to our enemies, just to communicate with them, in his words to "To look them in the eyes and say what needs to be said."

"How foolish, how inexperienced! They will use you as a tool for propaganda!" say the more experienced.

Well, as for me, if this is inexperience, then we need more people with less experience. Because the "inside-the-belt" position is a position of fear, not courage: fear of being used, fear of looking bad, and fear of failure. In their thinking you do not go in and talk to the enemy until your agents and minions have already wired the deal. Then the leaders go in, pretend to hold talks, and look like heroes. They give the example of

Nixon and the Chinese, where Kissinger brokered the deal in advance.

I say we need more heroes, not more people who want to look like heroes. Moral courage takes risks. It does the thing that is unexpected. Many of the people who criticize Obama's position claim, quite publicly, to be followers of Jesus. This confuses me. Jesus said,

"Others have told you, 'Love your neighbor and hate your enemy. But I tell you: Love your enemies and pray for those who hurt you."
(Matthew 5:43-44)

I am certain that "love your enemies" includes talking to them. It certainly precludes trying to kill them. It does not necessarily mean letting them have their way, but I think it does mean letting them have their say, and trust that the truth will be apparent.

I do not want to live in a theocracy. I do not expect politicians to run the country according to my religious opinions. I do not wish to legally impose my moral standards on others. But I wish people would stop proclaiming loyalty to the teachings of Jesus when they are really living out the philosophies that He specifically denounced. It would be more honest. It would be more clear.

But if they wanted a faith-based position for foreign policy, I have one to suggest. It is the words of George Fox, one of the founders of Quakerism. He had this advice for his followers traveling about the globe.

"Let all nations hear the sound by word or writing.
Spare no place, spare no tongue or pen, but be obedient
to the Lord God; go through the work, be valiant for
the truth upon the earth; and tread and trample down
what is contrary. Ye have the power, do not abuse
it...Keep down and low; and take heed of false joys that
will change...This is the word of the Lord God to you
all, and a charge to you all in the presence of the living
God; be patterns, be examples in all countries, places,
islands, nations wherever you come; that your carriage
and life may preach among all sorts of people, and to
them; then you will come to walk cheerfully over the
world, answering that of God in everyone; whereby in
them you may be a blessing, and make the witness of
God in them to bless you."
(G. Fox 1656)

To summarize Fox:

Proclaim the truth you know.

Use every method of communication possible.

Trample deceit. (Not trample deceived persons!)

Do not abuse your power.

Stay humble.

Live what you believe.

Presume that "the other" has God in them, as you do.

Heresy, you say? That of God in everyone? That of God
in Hugo Chavez? That of God in Osama Bin Laden?

I give you the Gospel of John, the first chapter the ninth verse.

"That was the true Light, (speaking clearly of Christ) which lights up every person that comes into the world."

John was not naïve about evil. He lived with the Romans; they killed all his fellow apostles before they got him. He lived through some of the most appalling persecutions, genocides, and atrocities that human kind has ever committed. And he believed that every human had innate goodness somewhere in them.

It is possible to speak truth, even to evil. But you have to speak.

This column was written in the summer of 2007. Barack Obama was barely a candidate. He had already earned my support.

* http://politicalticker.blogs.cnn.com/2007/07/29/obama-comment-fires-up-senior-clinton-official/

Tom Fox

He was one of us -- a Quaker -- a member of the Religious Society of Friends. I didn't know him personally, although I have known several people who have worked with Christian Peacemaker Teams. However, personal knowledge is not required for me to know this man. He embodied the testimonies we hold dear. He was a man changed by timeless truth, and being changed himself, he changed the world around him. Not content to just know the truth, he acted upon it.

My favorite thing about Tom was what he did during the Vietnam War. Unable, by conscience, to fight, he did not head for Canada – he did not go to jail. Instead he joined the Marine Band, and played his clarinet for them for 20 years. If I have my time and place right, he would have been playing "Hail to the Chief" for a president he mightily disagreed with. Some would see this as a contradiction or a compromise. I see it as witness to a thing we Quakers hold to be true. You **can** be present to the people you most disagree with. This is what it means to live out the Sermon on the Mount; to walk the extra mile; to stay engaged with someone even if it means getting your other cheek slapped.

This is why Tom went to Iraq -- to be present to people -- to join them physically in their trouble. He lived and worked for two years in a regular Baghdad neighborhood without guards or guns. I saw Anderson Cooper react on camera the other night, as he interviewed the clerk of Tom's Quaker meeting. "He lived **outside** the green zone without a guard!?" Yes, Anderson, he did. He taught peacemaking. He acted as an intermediary between incarcerated Iraqis and their families. He made friends. He was a non-anxious presence to occupier, insurgent, and the people caught in the middle.

"This is why the Father loves me, because I lay down my life - and I will take it back again. No one takes it away from me. On the contrary, I lay it down voluntarily. I have set it aside."
(The Gospel of John 10:17-18)

Tom Fox's life was not taken from him. Tom Fox laid his life down a long time ago. He surrendered it into the hands of the Divine. Because he knew it was safe there, he was able to walk unbound by fear, letting the Light within him control and impel him forward into the work of peace. Tom's life was safe in the hands of God before he went to Baghdad, it was safe in Baghdad, it was safe in captivity and it is safe now. The loss is ours to bear. But it is a temporary, perceptual loss, for we have also put our lives into the hands of the Divine, and so our lives and his remain together.

Tom did not fail in his task. I am sure that many of the tears shed this weekend were Iraqi tears. I am sure that many of the prayers that have been spoken have been spoken in languages other than English. I am certain that Tom had some effect on his captors, even if we do not see it. I am certain that his life will inspire a hundred others to pick up his work around the world. Task completed. Mission accomplished.

"Thee was faithful."

We pray and hope for Norman, Harmeet and James. We dedicate ourselves to their work.

Tom Fox was on a peacemaking mission with Christian Peacemaker Teams to Baghdad, when he and his three companions were kidnapped. Tom died by the hands of his captors on March 9, 2006. On March 2rd the other three were freed. This column was written between those two events. Tom was a member of Langley Hill Friends Meeting, Baltimore Yearly Meeting.

This is the only column in this book not written in the "So There I Was ..." format. Because I was not there. I can only hope and pray to be given the blessing of walking in Tom Fox's footprints.

Christian Peacemaker Teams - cpt.org

My Quaker Yoda

So there I was ...

sitting in the big-city hospital waiting room. My friend and mother, Vivian, had been rushed there from the Oregon Coast Quaker retreat center. She had suffered a heart attack followed by a massive stroke. She was in the middle of her eighth decade of life.

Vivian did not give birth to me in any natural fashion. That was apparent that morning because one of her natural born children was doing a fine and appropriate job of protecting her mother's repose and it was clear that I was not going to get in to see her. Absolutely appropriate, and painful as a red-hot poker.

I met Vivian when I was in my twenties. She is not the reason I became a Quaker, but she is a big piece of the reason that I stayed a Quaker. She was a big part of my accepting the process of becoming a recorded minister and a public Friend. She has been a mother to my soul.

She is hard to quantify or qualify. She is a little tiny thing, and getting tinier with time. Her eyes can still flash blue fire, but the rest of her has gone velvety soft, her muscles no longer fill out her skin. Her voice is almost always soft and gentle, but she has much of Christ in her, so she carries a power infinitely greater than its container. She laughs easily and often. She has rebuked me, and occasionally reigned me in. She has shed tears over me. She has breathed fire into me. She has salved my wounds.

She and her life partner, Hubert, facilitated the wedding for my first-born and her young man. Hubert is no larger than Vivian. My son-in-law is six foot something; my Emily is a foot shorter than he. It looked like the pastors of Hobbiton Friends Church were marrying off a favorite daughter to an elf-Lord. But my son-in-law, an observant young man, nailed the best ever description of our Vivian.

"I get it now," he said. "Vivian is Yoda – she's your Jedi master."

Vivian put me on the road to spiritual maturity, and she has walked that road before me. She has always made time to teach me when I need it. The following is what I have learned from her by word and observation.

Our value as children of God does not depend on our spiritual maturity - grandparents do not have more intrinsic worth than the babies - but neither are they less valuable. So it is with spiritual maturity. It is merely the natural consequence of time spent in the presence of the Holy One, like age is the natural consequence of life. But maturity is a need of, and a blessing to, the Body of Christ. It can be sought, but not acquired. The goal must be Christ - the by-product is maturity.

Maturity can be seen in terms of Freedom. We were created to be free. Christ died and rose to restore us to a place of freedom. Spiritual maturity is the presence of spiritual freedom and the absence of spiritual slavery.

A spiritually mature person is free to bring pleasure to others, without needing to make them happy all the time.

A free Christian can be honest;they will know how to be respectfully honest with their thoughts, behaviors, and feelings.

They will not need to revise the past to feed their ego or ease their pain.

They will be free to follow their path and change course when it seems wise to them.

They will be free to listen to God and to follow.

They will be free from the slavery of what people will think of them.

They will be free from a morbid fear of rejection.

They will be free from the need to collect second-hand information about the thoughts, words, and actions of others as a way to buttress their own opinions and self-esteem.

They will be free to bless those who disagree with them.

They will be free from the need to correct all misconceptions that others may have of them.

They will be free to trust that Christ will work in others as He works in them.

They will be free from the need to make others "get it."

They will be free to let go when appropriate, to speak when appropriate, and to act when appropriate.

They will be free to take personal responsibility for all their thoughts, and behaviors, and feelings.

They will be free to ask for, and then accept, criticism from trusted guides.

They will be free to apologize and make amends where possible.

All these things I learned from Christ through Vivian. I have seen her live them out. She will, of course, discount this when she reads this because she has also mastered humility.

Yes, she will read this. She was in a hospital with some mighty fine doctors. After two hours of no blood flow to the entire left half of her brain, they managed to surgically remove the blood clot. Then they put in a pacemaker. Shortly thereafter, she opened her eyes and looked at Hubert and said.

"Hubert, you've been in those clothes for three days now, don't you think you ought to change?"

Dangerous Quakers

So there I was...

feeling dangerous. I could have taken my great big motorcycle out for a fast run, but that didn't feel dangerous enough. I was tired of my government, my society. I could have joined the large rally at the State Capitol a few blocks from my house, "Si, Se Puede!" but they seemed to have things under control and did not need me. I whipped a few e-mails off to my congressional representatives about torture and detainment without legal recourse and rendition, but it did not cool the fire in my belly. I needed to do something way outside the bell curve, something so radical that if everyone followed my lead, it would shake foundations, topple governments, create societal chaos – I was in that kind of mood. So this is what I did. First, I took a chunk of money that I was planning to use for a nice shopping excursion and sent it to a group in the third world. I thereby robbed the US economy of that money and I robbed the US government of the taxes on that money. Then, I went out and put into the hands of a young person a piece of paper that they could use to make sure that the US military could not aim its recruitment lies in their direction. Then to cap the day, I went to meeting for worship, and I, the preacher did not preach. I did not tell them what to think, I did not tell them what to believe. We sat silently and let God talk to the folks completely without theological middlemen.

You see, I am a dangerous Quaker. You have heard about us I am sure. Over at the New York Times* they report that Senator Patrick Leahy (D-Vermont) was recently asking the FBI why they were spying on groups like the Quakers and the Raging Grannies. Apparently there were about a hundred anti-war groups that were spied on that could have been mentioned. I suspect that the Quakers and the Raging Grannies got named are because they seemed so patently and ridiculously undangerous. With all due respect Mr. Senator, if you think that an enraged grandmother is not a dangerous thing, you have never seen one. And please, do not count the Quakers out yet.

In addition to the FBI, the Department of Defense and the NSA have been spying on us. Apparently they haven't found anything worthy of detention or harassment, yet. I feel kind of sorry for these guys. They have fallen on hard times. Their info is all swiss-cheesy. So as an act of charity, I am going to make it a little easier on them. Tune in your web data miners to this station and stay tuned. I cannot and **do not** speak for all Quakers. But I can speak for me. I am about to give you some solid intelligence. Listen up!

The Top Ten Reasons why I am a dangerous Quaker and should be watched carefully.

1- I believe that there is a seed of God and goodness in everyone. It may be small, starved, buried and stepped on, but it is there, and can be reached under the right circumstances. This includes Osama Bin Laden, Hugo Chavez and Fidel Castro. The right circumstances for reaching that goodness does not include bombings and assassination attempts.

2 - I cannot in good conscience say the Pledge of Allegiance. My patriotism is expressed through informed voting and paying my taxes; but my allegiance is to a Kingdom not of this world. I pledge to no other. Even if I could pledge my allegiance to this country, I could not say **that** pledge because I attempt to only say true things and it includes the patent and obvious falsehoods that we are "One nation under God" and that there is "Liberty and justice for all." This, I have not observed to be true.

3 - I cannot swear an oath in court, not on the Bible or any other book. I take that book very seriously and that book contains the instruction to not swear oaths because it implies that you have two standards of truth. That book says to let your "yes" be "yes" and your "no" be "no", and leave it at that.

4 - I believe that **all** war is incompatible with the teachings of Jesus. He said that we were to love our enemies, and I think that this meant at the very least that you should not kill them. Our present war is immoral, as has been every other war; and yes, I include World War II and the American Revolution in that list.

5 – I do not believe in the death penalty. We may indeed need to keep some citizens safely locked up for life. But I would not put any human to death as a consequence of crime. And that includes Timothy

McVeigh or Ted Bundy. It's the "Love your enemies" thing again.

6 – I respect my fellow voter's rights to disagree with me; to fund and support a military. But I think that military recruiting, like other sinful behavior, should be limited to consenting adults. It should be illegal to aim military recruiting at secondary school students.

7 – I do not believe in living beyond my means. This is also in the teachings of Jesus on the subject of simplicity. Our Household is presently living with no consumer debt beyond our house. I hope to keep it that way. I am not a very simple Quaker; many do much better than me in this spiritual discipline. But if everyone in the US shopped even as liberally as I do, the economy would crash, big and bad.

8 – I try to send as much of my money as possible outside of the US economy. I think we should be poorer and the poor nations should be richer. I do this by supporting organizations that reduce poverty. I do not pay much attention to whether or not the people helped, or their governments, agree with US foreign policy. The cool subversive benefit of this is that the government lets me forego taxes on this money, which means less money for the military and other projects of which I do not approve.

9 – I am not actually keen on national borders in general. I am not worried about illegal immigration from Mexico. Fine folks, by and large. Figure out how to tax them. I would gleefully support a national sales

tax that paid for universal health care and schools. I think the national anthem sounds great in Spanish.

10 – I think that informed, non-violent, conscience driven dissent is extremely patriotic. I also think that it is sexy.

So there you go guys. I'm sure that you know my numbers. Feel free to check in regularly. The link below is my Quaker church. You would be most welcome to spy on and worship with us any Sunday.

Freedom Friends Church – freedomfriends.org

*http://www.nytimes.com/2006/05/02/washington/02cnd-fbi.html?_r=2&hp&ex=1146628800&en=0a9949500d2da 5cb&ei=5094&partner=homepage&oref=slogin

Noisy Quakers

"Be still and know that I am God."
(Psalm 46:10)

So there I was ...

sitting in a very noisy Quaker meeting.

For some of us, this is unusual. Quakers are known for having a big taste for quiet. We practice a listening spirituality. Whatever else we do, the core of our worship is supposed to be listening to the present Christ and if we are given a message for the community we are supposed to speak it. Because we have been around for 350 years with no centralized church government, the practice of this has become extremely divergent. African Friends sing, loudly and long, often dance, and then listen to the present Christ discerned by the designated preacher, some American meetings also follow this practice. At the other extreme you will find British meetings that will actually boast about how many decades it has been since anyone spoke in meeting – they have elevated the listening process, and appear to have forgotten the purpose of the listening. There is an urban American meeting that in the mid-1800s would go out on Sunday morning and put straw over the cobblestones of the street so as to muffle the hoof beats of passing horses. Some of us like quiet just that much. The majority of Quaker meetings and churches include some quantity of sitting still, being quiet, and listening. It is not always easy. It is counter-cultural. It makes many people uncomfortable.

It's not rock and roll, but we like it.

The meeting I usually attend is a Quaker hybrid. We sing a little. We pray out loud a bit. Then we settle down, and shut up. Someone usually receives a message to speak, often several someones. The messages are usually right on target. We like the peace that we get between the messages. Most of the people in the room are new Quakers; they are acquiring a taste for the silence.

One morning recently two strangers walked in. A mother and an early teenage son. The son looked around. He looked panic stricken. He turned to his mom and said loudly. "Oh **no**! Not church! Don't want church!" The boy had autism. I greeted the mother and she said to me, "This may not work; we may not be able to stay." I said, "Please try, you are welcome here. Your son is welcome here."

Our room is pretty small. We sit facing each other in concentric semi-circles. There isn't really any place to hide. The mother took her son and sat on what constitutes the backbench. The boy was not happy. He did not want to stay. The mother tried several tricks to get him to settle. He vocalized, every few seconds, for the next hour.

We sang. The boy declared "No sad songs!"

We prayed. The boy said "No. No No. No church!"

We settled into silence. The boy moaned, clucked, muttered, and talked.

"Don't wanna be quiet!" he called out.

After a few minutes, some other vocal ministry arose. It was sweet. It was true. It was just what Jesus would have said. It didn't directly address the situation; it addressed the needs of the meeting. The boy said "Good one!" and proceeded to yip.

After a few more minutes, a scripture passage was raised. The boy crowed.

I experienced what some Quakers call "gathering" it is a deepening of the silence. A kind of mystical feeling of the bottom dropping out of the meeting. A transcendence. A visceral experience of the presence of God. It was a gathered non-silence.

The time passed swiftly.

The meeting rose. Friends greeted the mother and the boy. The mother attempted to apologize. No one was having any of that. We knew that we had experienced a first rate Quaker meeting. We know that the purpose of meeting is not to escape from the world to a place quiet enough to listen, but to learn to listen well enough that we can listen anywhere, under any conditions. It had been a good and rewarding morning's practicum. We were grateful. There was not a single kvetcher, not a single grumbler, not then, not later.

One of those present was a new attender, a new Christian, a new Quaker. She is a transgendered woman. She has lots of tattoos. She was checking us out, watchful.

She had been burned by church people. She walked up to me after meeting and said,

"Well, hmm. I guess you really mean it. I guess everyone really is welcome, wow. Walking the talk, hmm."

God told the psalmist, "*Be still and know that I am God.*" Quakers like that verse. Many think the stillness referred to means silence. It does not. The Hebrew verb means to relax, let go, stop trying so hard, release. In order to see God, you have to stop striving, stop relying on your own strength. You have to give up your notions of how things should be. You have to let go of preferences and pet peeves. You have to open yourself up to the uncomfortable.

Then God shows up.

Proselyphobia

So there I was ...

going door-to-door selling religion. Well, actually I wasn't going door to door, I was sitting under a tree lying about going door-to-door.

I was at a youth camp of the Christian denomination of my childhood. Despite the fact that many of us were showing clear signs of spiritual doubt, confusion, and obvious natural and spiritual immaturity, the powers-that-be decided that they should send us out into the neighboring community as representatives of the faith.

I do not know what they were thinking.

As it was the only way to get to the Saturday night watermelon feed and hayride, I decided to play along. But when it came down to it – time to knock on a door and ask somebody if they wanted to meet Jesus – I just couldn't do it. I didn't have any Jesus to introduce them to. Even as a backslider I had more integrity than that.

But there was a form to fill out, reporting on the result at each house on my assignment, so I ditched my partner on the pretense that this would go quicker if we split up, and then I bought a soda, and sat down under a tree and made up responses. Lying to my youth leaders seemed like a better idea than lying to unbelievers. I had another choice, of course, lie to nobody, and "come out" as the apostate I was, but that would have certainly gotten back to my mother and I was not up to that.

I think this experience was the genesis of my prosely-phobia.

Yes, that's right, proselyphobia - the fear of recruitment - especially religious recruitment. I have this fear and perhaps so do you. It is common among religious people, even people whose religion teaches that re-cruitment is critical and mandatory. It is equally common among people who think their faith is a good one among equals. It is common.

The problem for me is that I am called to be an evan-gelist. It is an inconvenient phobia for me to have. You see, these days I don't think respectful religious re-cruitment is inherently bad. These days I have some-thing real to share. I actually think that I carry the following wonderful truth around in my back pocket.

There is a God. This God loves you. You can have immediate, constant access to this God. This God will show up and teach you. This God became human in the person of Jesus of Nazareth. Because of Him you do not have to live in captivity to, or fear of, **anything**.

I carry this around, I know it experientially, and I believe that people around me are literally dying for the want of it. They die from addiction, from loneliness, from despair, from idolatry. I think that what I carry around would save lives. And still, I am at times afraid to share what I have with them.

I think part of my fear comes from really, seriously, not wanting to be associated with people who have done nasty, coercive, sometimes violent recruitment. The proselytizing that they attempted to train me in as a youth was merely annoying in comparison, but I don't want to be associated with that either.

But if you divided the whole world up into the teams of believers, I would have to choose the team that includes Johnny Cash, Joseph Shabalala, Bono, and Mother Theresa, even if I have to have Jim Dobson and the Spanish Inquisition on my side. Any other team is just not my home.

I am pretty sure that the sub-group I hang out with now, the Quakers, would never, under any circumstances use violence to force people to convert. The worst behavior that I have witnessed among them is emotional manipulation designed to provoke a cathartic convincement, and even that has gone out of style. And even the most ardent promoters of using emotion to get at faith would admit that it is a useless endeavor unless the soul is ready for God. Yet this over-emotional approach has left many Friends proselyphobic.

At the other end of the Quaker spectrum, some Friends think that it is offensive to even say to somebody that you think they should consider a life of faith lived the way we live it. These same folks often have no trouble loudly proclaiming their political beliefs in the streets, but they would never carry a picket for Jesus or Quakerism. It would just seem gauche. So they talk about peace, and justice but not about God. And because they don't like to promote what they have, they are hard to find sometimes.

I have parked my buggy between these two ends. I believe that people are free - that they are grown-ups, mostly. We live in a society teeming with ideas and experiences. I am not offended when someone offers an idea or an experience to me. Why should I be afraid to offer mine? If I offer to share the source of my hope, it is ok with me if you say "yes", "no", or "tell me more."

When I meet a person who has a deep, practical working faith, I usually want to learn from them. I feel no need to try and talk them out of what is obviously working, however they name it. But the reality is that many people around me don't seem to have that intimate connection to the Divine. And I do. And I know how I got it. And I don't think that it is hard to get. Yet I often say little or nothing about what I know.

I know that I am afraid of false advertising. People promise stupid stuff in the name of religion, like "This faith path will solve all your problems, or automatically make you rich and healthy." This is a lie, but faith does have its benefits. You will never be truly alone. You can seek and find meaning. I have learned to talk about faith honestly, but still I hesitate.

I know that I am afraid of hypocrisy. I mean, I am a screw-up, always have been, always will be. Do you know how afraid I am of becoming a TV evangelist? I don't even like people to take my picture, let alone videotape me. I have an uncanny ability to cause videotaping systems to malfunction. But actually, faith has made me less of a hypocrite, not more of one. There are parts of my life I can let you see and imitate. There are parts where you might want to find a better model, but I know one from the other. Yet at times I hesitate to share even the good parts.

I know that I am plagued by occasional deep doubt. What if I am a lot more delusional than I think I am? What if I have dedicated my life to the playing of a pretend game, and am encouraging others to join me? What if the present Christ is just an elaborate imaginary friend? These moments come, yes they do. But they never stay, because it takes much more energy to sustain the doubts than to sustain the belief. I always relax back into faith. I love better from faith. I laugh better from faith. Everything that is good about me is better from the place of faith. My doubts don't disqualify my testimony; they make it stand out in clarity.

Like all phobias, proselyphobia does not evaporate in the face of logical argument. It can only be conquered by learning to relax in the face of that which you fear. I am working on my proselyphobia. I have made up my mind to speak what I know at every chance I get. I am learning to take responsibility only for my testimony, not the effect my testimony has on the world – that is God's job, not mine. I am choosing to speak from my own experience, flawed example, though I am, or perhaps especially because I am a flawed example.

I am getting over it.

Selling Fear, Greed and Falsehood

So there I was ...

on my front porch. I live in a nice old school kind of neighborhood. The housing is mixed, the mature trees are breaking up the sidewalks, front porches often have furniture, the people walking by will usually greet you, and the mosquitoes being not too bad, nothing is screened in. This I like.

Being that kind of neighborhood, we have people going door to door. The occasional uniformed cookie sales-person still pulls a flexible flyer up the sidewalk – I would expect that the devil himself would be selling thin mints – they are that tempting. We get religious people, usually the Witnesses or the Mormons – I try and be polite. Oregon has a political climate that makes it easy to get things on the ballots so we get petitioners, some of them fervent volunteers and some paid by the signature. I won't sign when they are doing it for the bucks. And we get regular salespeople of several varieties. Except for the cookie imps, I refuse sales at my front door; I prefer to decide when I am going to shop.

Then up walked this young man, he found me in a pretty good mood, and he was a pretty boy. College vacation job, no doubt. So I was a little more tolerant than usual.

"Hi! Could I please ask you a question?"

(Points for not calling me ma'am – points for saying please.)

"Oh, sure, ask away, but I may not answer."

"Do you rent or own this home?"

"Well, that's a mighty personal question to ask a stranger."

Oh, I'm sorry. I'm Dan and I'm with Blah Blah Security Systems."

"Nice, to meet you Dan. I'm Peggy. Selling security then?"

"Oh no, I'm not selling anything today, I am the point man for our company and today I am just out gathering marketing research. But we are concerned with security."

Then he launched into a spiel about the dangers of living in "crime soaked" Salem, Oregon. It was pretty funny. I smiled a lot, but didn't quite laugh. See top paragraph about front porch living – until last year when the dog died, I never had a key to my own house. I mostly didn't lock it when I was away and cannot conceive of locking it while I am home and awake. We lock the doors at night, but my kids know which windows never get locked. Eventually, I interrupted Dan.

"Son, for the sake of honesty, I need to tell you that you are actually wasting your time here on this porch."

"Aren't you concerned about security?"

"Never felt safer anywhere, anytime."

I didn't bother to tell him about my recent trip to a war zone, or the fact that I pack my sense of safety with me, so that I almost never feel less safe either. He tried to restart the line.

"Peggy, a lot of your neighbors are worried about their security."

OK – then I laughed.

"Son, you aren't going to sell me a security system."

"Ah, but see here's the thing! I am not trying to sell you a security system today. We are just trying to make a presence in the neighborhood. We would like to **pay you** to put our sign in your window for your neighbors to see. Then, when our sales people come around, folks will have seen the name, and will feel like if you trust our company with your safety then maybe they should too. And the thieves will **think** you have the system, so it will deter them as well. Cool huh?"

"So you think false advertising is cool? Really?"

"Nothing false about it!"

"I am not afraid of crime, but you want me to pretend that I am so that my neighbors sense of concern will rise, and they will think that I have installed this system, even though I haven't, and I am going to try and fake out the thieves, and you want me to do this for money, and you don't call that false?"

Danny boy was starting to look a wee bit confused.

For the third time I tried the simple truth.

"Truly, Dan, you are actually talking to the wrong woman, I can't say it any plainer than that. Have a nice day, son."

I walked in the house.

"Don't you even want to know how much we will pay you?!?!" Dan shouted after me.

"No, I don't, it makes no difference."

Dan went down the stairs, confused, mildly disturbed, dejected.

Poor Dan, he had his pitch down so nicely. I wonder how transparent they were at sales-boy school. Did they tell him that they were selling on the two pillars of fear and greed? I wonder if they had numbers for how many people are motivated by these things. He certainly was presuming that I was. He was confused when it did not work.

Motivation – that which moves you – that which underlies your actions – this is a good thing to be acquainted with. If you know what moves you, and even better, if you can influence or even choose what moves you, you will have the power to resist those who would move you in their own interests.

But to look at your own motivations you have to be willing to look at your own dark side. Young Dan had no idea that the middle aged lady before him would be much more moved by power and control than by fear and greed. But even if he had, it would not have done him much good because I know those things about myself. I have taken them off auto-pilot and cruise control. I have surrendered them to a higher power. That's my security system. If they get the better of me, it is not without plenty of warning, plenty of chances to turn another way. I am not likely to confuse them with better motivations like compassion and loyalty as I would have in the past. I am not perfectly secure from the darkness, but I am not an easy target. I bet my soul has a sign in the window.

I walked around my neighborhood last evening. I could not find a single house with the security company sign in their window. I am proud to live in this neighborhood. I feel kind of sorry for Dan, but we all have our lessons to learn.

Waiting Worship

So there I was...

at the airport. Waiting. I was early. I had planned that. Then I became earlier as my expected person was delayed once, twice, and then three times. I ended up with eight hours of wait time.

I was able to see the blessing in it pretty quickly since it was 102 degrees outside and the airport had refrigerated air. I had the ability to purchase a good meal and a good book, and I like the airport.

It is a great place to people watch. Every type of person on every type of business passes through. The extremely elderly and newborn babes are assisted on their way. Business, commercial, and personal, is pursued with determination. The entire repertoire of human drama gets replayed every hour or so, re-cast with each arriving plane.

As a bit of an empath, I have a distinct seating preference. I stay away from the screening and departure area if I have a choice. People there are sad, leaving or being left. They are anxious and in a hurry. They are frustrated and sometimes angry at all the security nonsense.

I like waiting in the arrivals lounge. The anxiety is the good kind. It builds and builds as people wait, watching the clock and the corridor until it bursts in an explosion of joy when they see the much-anticipated one.

"Mommy!!!!" screamed the three year old who escaped dad, got neatly around the guard and into his mother's arms, and everybody, including the security guard, smiled.

Grandmas, babies, soldiers home from war. Nothing stronger than the wave of relief coming off the weary young mother traveling with three under five, when she sees her parents waiting to help – "Made it, made it, worth it already!" The dramas are the same regardless of ethnicity or class. It's all pretty intoxicating.

I spent a lot of time watching one young man. Twentyish, cool in a 70s sort of way; self-possessed, long curly hair, a neat beard, dark shades. He's wearing baggy jeans, but a clean shirt – probably his best shirt. It had buttons.

He paced, checking the time on his cell phone, checking the arrivals board way too often. He was wise enough to have discovered an important life secret. Always bring flowers to the airport. The flowers were purple daisies – dyed – poor man's flowers, which made him more endearing.

He held the flowers like a straight man holds flowers. Blooms down, drooping, casual, light grip, like he was carrying a bat up to the plate. He doesn't care about the stupid flowers. He cares a lot about the girl.

I wait with him, wondering what she will look like. Wondering if she loves him as much as he loves her. Hoping she hasn't missed her connection. Would she have preferred the one red rose? Hope, belief, doubt, swirling around him like a cyclone.

The wait is getting to him. He presses one hand on his heart, and blows out a deep shuddering stress-filled breath. He adjusts himself – hold on, tiger. Then his phone rings and ends his agony. She is on the ground and couldn't walk the length of the concourse without calling him. He grins, and charges the gate just like the three year old.

She's pretty – very pretty – and runs to meet him. Hugs, hugs, rocking hugs, and he kisses her on the forehead. Then he remembers the flowers. Of course she likes them.

Waiting is so holy. Anticipation is so holy.
Joy is so holy.

We Quakers say that we practice "waiting worship". We sit, silent, waiting, expecting the present Christ to arrive. Our meetings are sacred arrivals lounges, or they should be. I wonder how often we experience the level and quality of anticipation and joy that you see at the airport.

Maybe we should bring flowers.

Where I Came From

I was born in Chicago, Illinois on the last day of 1957. My parents loved and served a God they shared, and then each other. My two brothers and I knew where we stood, and it was OK. We were barely middle class, but we had good schools. Our family life revolved around a small church of the Holiness variety. I learned a great deal from my parents, most of it good and useful. I also learned a great deal from the religious culture, less consistently good, but as I age I find ways to treasure even the most difficult of those lessons.

The Beauty in Darkness

So there I was ...

six years old – on a family summer vacation in a cabin by a lake in Wisconsin. I was tucked into a warm bed on a back sleeping porch. It had been a warm August day, but the summer night air was decidedly cool. I had played myself into righteous childhood exhaustion. My parents were sleeping in another room - my brothers were nearby. There were no locks on the doors. All was quiet, and with no moon that night, stunningly dark.

Sleeping deeply, at first I was not even aware as the strong male hands folded the blankets under me, and lifted me from the bed. Groggy, when the voice whispered "Shush, don't wake anyone." I obeyed.

It was only when I was carried out the back porch door, and slipped out into the dark woods, that I realized what a strange thing was going on. I looked up into the face of the man carrying me.

"Daddy, why are we out in the woods in the middle of the night?"

"I've got something important to show you, Peg."

Good enough for me. I think I snoozed some more as he walked on. Up a hill and into a clearing.

"Daddy, it's cold!"

"I know, Honey. Look up."

He cradled me in his arms and I looked up into the night sky. There was a meteor shower going on – the Perseid meteor shower to be exact. And it was a good show that year. Stars rocketed like fireworks across the heavens.

"Wow, the stars are running around!"

"Peggy, I want you always to remember this – sometimes you have to go out into the dark and the cold to see the really beautiful things that God has to show you."

I remember.

Being as we are human, mortal, fragile, stuck in time and space, we tend to have human, fragile, and stuck values. Pain is bad – pleasure is good. Life is good – death is bad. Wealth is good – poverty is bad, and so on.

Unable to do much in the way of comprehending the actuality of God, we tend to project upon the Divine our own values. Surely God agrees with us, wants for us what we want, right?

I think perhaps not.

Here's what I have observed about God's apparent values:

I think God cares more about beauty than comfort.
I think God cares more about courage than safety.
I think God cares more about freedom than good behavior.
I think God cares more about sacrifice than suffering.

I think God cares more about generosity that wealth.
I think God cares more about honor than position.
I think God cares more about truth than harmony.
I think God cares more about grace than rewards or
punishment.

I think the list goes on.

To see the things that God cares about, you have to go
into some pretty col, dark places of human behavior.
War is evil – in every case, but in the dark, joyless,
airless mineshafts of war there are sometimes found
diamonds of human nobility, honor, and sacrifice that
stand out more brilliantly for the despicable back-
ground.

In the midst of our cold harsh treatment of the home-
less and the mentally ill, I have seen kindness and
courage. I have camped out in the Valley of the Shadow
of Death, and while the amenities are nothing to write
home about, there is a little restaurant there called "In
the Presence of My Enemies", where the Maitre d' is
Jesus and the kitchen is full of cooking angels. You can
always get a table there. No reservations required.

I have seen sick and suffering children preach sermons
of simple hope and truth that Spurgeon and Dr. King
could not touch. If it were up to me, no children would
ever suffer. It appears to me that God wants to hear
them preach.

I hear people say, "I don't want a God who claims to be loving but allows this stuff to happen!" I get this. But I honestly don't think we get to pick our God. I think we get to pick our response to God. I think we get to spend our lives aligning our values (or not) to a cosmic set of values in which death and pain are no longer relevant. Old father Job expressed this when he said

Though you slay me, yet shall I trust you.(13:15).

I choose to believe that God's values are better than mine, because I have seen the beauty in the darkness.

I remember, Dad.

The Green Mile

So there I was ...

walking the green mile.

OK, it wasn't a mile, it just seemed like it. But the long corridor was a sort of turquoise green. I wasn't actually condemned to death, though for a second grader I might as well have been. Dead little girl walking, and worse, I had to do it every Tuesday afternoon for all of second grade.

The call came at two p.m. every Tuesday, just before all the other kids went to recess. My teacher, Miss Cartier tried to be as subtle as possible, sidling up to my desk and whispering, "Peggy, it's time." But it didn't matter because all the kids knew where I was going. They snickered behind their hands, and giggled as I got up from my seat and left the room. I was nervous and often managed to kick something or bump into something on the way out. Kids would stick their foot out and try to trip me if the teacher took her eyes off me. Miss Cartier didn't let them get away with any words, but it didn't matter, because there was after school, and before school, and other recesses to get the taunts in. I was labeled for the rest of grade school.

I was walking down to what the kids at school called the "retard room." Even in 1965 nobody was allowed to call it that in front of teachers or staff, it was officially the classroom for the "handicapped" children. But on the playground that is what they called it, and they called me a "retard."

I actually got to know the kids in that classroom. Some of them spent their whole days there. Some kids assigned to that class spent part of their days in a regular classroom. It was a pretty progressive school district. Some of them had physical difficulties, some had developmental difficulties, and some of them didn't seem all that different from the kids in the regular classes.

I was pigeon-toed. Seriously pigeon-toed. I tripped over my own feet all the time. I scuffed my Mary Jane's all to death. They tried making me wear those special stiff high shoes, but they didn't help. So I got sent to Miss Belknap the physical rehab teacher.

Here's what the other kids didn't know. The long walk down the green hall was hell, but heaven was just on the other side of the door to Miss Belknap's room. The room was full of giant toys and gymnastics equipment. She wore sneakers and shorts while all the other teachers were in heels and dresses. She was kinda loud, and funny, and she was pretty masculine for a lady. She called me "Girly." I didn't know anybody else like her. But she liked me. I think she liked all her kids. When I walked in the door she welcomed me, like a beloved lost lamb. As if she was surprised to see me. As if I was the best part of her day. She was the best part of my week.

She taught me how to walk. How to turn my hips so that my toes would go straight. How to tuck in my tiny little butt so that my hips would open out. We practiced many walks, we walked like ducks, we walked like cowboys. She would have me put my hands behind my back as if they were tied and I would pretend to walk the plank – with plenty of pirate talk to go with it. We laughed a lot. Wednesday mornings during second grade I was always a little sore. I remember one day in the spring when she was pretty pleased with me and she said, "Well, we could quit now, Girly, but as long as we've taught you to walk straight, we might as well teach you how to walk pretty." I did not object. Then I spent a few weeks walking like Miss America with a crown on my head. If they would have let me stay with Miss Belknap for the three R's I would have stayed. Miss Belknap was my secret treasure.

There is a stanza in the Serenity prayer attributed to Reinhold Niebuhr that goes

Living one day at a time;

Enjoying one moment at a time;

Accepting hardship

As the pathway to peace.

I learned the truth of that every Tuesday in second grade. After the mocking there was grace. After the loneliness there was kind attention. After the pain came fun. I could have let the humiliation ruin the joy, but I didn't. And in my memory the grace is huge and lively and the persecution is ghostly and pale.

Perspective is a choice.

So there I was ten years later, 1975, in the grocery on an errand for my mother. I whizzed around a corner in my three-inch platform sandals and mini skirt. I heard a loud voice from the back of the store yell,

"Stop right there! – Is that you Peggy? Peggy Senger?

I executed a perfect pivot turn and faced Miss Belknap, now a retired teacher. I grinned. She whistled a loud wolf whistle as all the patrons of the store turned and looked.

"Look at that walk! Look at that pretty, humdinger of a walk! Give me a bit more, Girly!"

So I gave her my best strut and then a hug and we laughed. And she said,

"Well, Girly, when you walk that plank they are gonna remember the last thing they see! Go get 'em."

So I did.

Speaking Truth to Power

So there I was ...

sitting in a Wednesday night Bible study. I was a very young adolescent. The church was small, Midwestern, Christian and conservative. A volunteer churchman was teaching the mixed class of adults and teens that muggy summer night. He was going on about the creation story in Genesis with a special emphasis on the place of man and woman in the story. He was trying to make the point that because man was made first that this clearly put him in charge. I spoke up and said something that indicated that I didn't think this was very good exegesis. This brought the undivided attention of teacherman who said;

"Really, Miss Peggy; and why, then, do you think that God made man first?"

"I dunno; if at first you don't succeed, try, try again?"

I don't remember his response, although I think there was minor sputtering involved. I do remember that my mother stifled a laugh, and shot me a look. I expected that look to involve disapproval. I was surprised to see amusement, and maybe a little bit of pride in my mother's eyes. At the time she said nothing. Later she spoke to me, in private, and her words were about refraining from the temptation to humiliate and mock people in public.

You see, my father was a strong, good man – a natural born leader. But he did not rule my mother. She had a sense of self, rooted in God's love for her, and it could not be shaken, oppressed or ruled. She was my father's – any man's – true equal. At her breast I got not only physical antibodies, but also spiritual and emotional antibodies. I grew up resistant to oppression. I learned to listen, but I let no one do my thinking for me. I found my voice early. I practiced using it until it became strong and even occasionally disciplined.

I learned my Bible, and I learned it well, but I also learned that the purpose of religious education is not the indoctrination of beliefs, but the inoculation of invincibility.

A couple of decades later I found myself sitting in the anteroom of a guitar studio. I was eavesdropping on my 13 year old daughter and her wise, gentle, and gifted guitar teacher. Mr. Walt had student recitals twice a year. Emily loved her guitar and loved Mr. Walt, but hated recitals. At the age of eight she just went along with it, by ten she was resisting, but could be bribed. At early adolescence she found her voice – she told me that she wasn't going to play in this year's recital, and none of my tricks worked. I liked the recitals. I liked seeing my beautiful child shine. I sat there hoping that Walt would talk her into it, one more time. He asked, he cajoled, he tried minor guilt and gentle manipulation. Emily held her ground.

Then my thinking took a radical shift -- I felt my own, now deceased, mother's presence in the room, and she was rooting for Emily. I realized that my daughter was holding to her sense of self in the face of the temptation to please someone she respected, and wanted to please, but with whom she disagreed. I changed my allegiance.

Emily continued to play her guitar but never played in another recital. The inoculation took; like her mother and grandmother before her – she was and is invincible – any time she wishes to be.

Protection

So there I was ...

selling insurance door to door. Which was odd because I was fourteen years old.

It was about a week before Halloween. I was the president of the church youth group. This was not a powerful or prestigious position since it was a small church and there were about six teenagers. I was technically apostate at the time, but mostly no one knew it. I had really good parents, and I not only didn't want to break their hearts with my apostasy, I was also hoping they would pay for college. Being in charge of the youth group meant that I had some influence over the level of religiosity, and could keep it to forms my hypocrisy could tolerate. A kind of theological détente.

Everybody knows that youth groups can only have fun if they have some cash to spend. It was part of my job to think up fund-raisers. I wanted to do something fresh. Something that actually provided a useful service to the community. Something that didn't involve too much manual labor. Then the light bulb went on. We would sell window-egg insurance.

Some bad kids (not us) used the "trick" part of "trick or treat" to throw eggs at houses. It was common enough that local grocers would watch out for any kid trying to buy eggs in bulk in late October. My brilliant idea was to go door-to-door selling an insurance policy for a $1 premium. If your house got egged you call our hotline and we send a nice kid out immediately to wash your windows. I figured that most housewives would think it was a good deal and that most houses wouldn't get egged, and that we would clean up (so to speak). I didn't bother to run the idea past any adults. I printed up the flyers and coupons and the group of us set out to sell.

To our great disappointment, we made no sales – none. Some ladies just stared at us. Some ladies yelled at us like we were hooligans. "No. Ma'am, we are here to **protect** you from the hooligans!" We regrouped – confused.

I went to my afternoon job as a soda jerk in the local ice cream parlor. I sat in the back room with Robert, the old black man who washed dishes for the restaurant. I told him my troubles. Then he laughed himself off his chair, he laughed so hard he cried. Then he carefully explained to me the concept of a protection racket. See, we lived in a neighborhood heavily populated by the higher levels of the Chicago mob. Robert asked me if I had tried to sell my insurance at the home of Tony Accardo – a few blocks away. "Jeez, Robert, I'm not a **moron**, nobody would egg Tony Accardo's house!" At fourteen I knew about the mob, I just didn't understand the finer points of their day to day rackets.

So here is what Robert taught me. "protection" was a process whereby the wise guys in the area "watched" your home, business, or auto in exchange for money that you paid them so that they would refrain from vandalizing you home, business, or auto.

We did a bake sale instead.

Oddly enough, this is pretty much what I got out of my early theological education. If you did enough stuff for God (The preferred currency), God would refrain from blasting you. I am not saying that my parents taught me this, they didn't, but it was a fairly common theme in the church culture I lived in.

Then I noticed that this God was a pretty crummy wise guy. He often appeared to blast good people anyway. A God less honorable than the Mob was not a God I wanted. Hence the apostasy.

Eventually, a truly weird thing happened. I met the Lover of my soul, the present Christ and I found out that some really malicious slander and libel had been committed against Him, but that He was way too gentle to blast anybody over it, although the power to do so seemed to be there.

Jesus is not a racketeer. I came to understand His protection as the state of being, in which, surrounded by His love, other things, including some pretty major hurts, begin to heal and rapidly lose their power over me. Some things that ought to hurt don't even bother me anymore. His Love has become my armor.

We started to travel together, and sometimes, (Just to mess with my head, I think), He started to provide some pretty amazing incidents of physical protection. Most of these events have happened when I was participating with Him in His hobbies (life transformation, wound healing, captive freeing, etc.) So there I was again, back at the beginning, doing cool stuff, for and with Him, and there He is protecting me from blasts. But from the inside, it had none of the feel of a scam.

It is also a mystery to me, unexplainable, because sometimes the protection does not **seem** to be there, and many people have never experienced it at all. Yet He assures me, it is there all the same. We argue about this a bit.

Being a wee bit of a risk taker, I occasionally test the limits of this protection. I have not yet succeeded in outrunning it. Mostly I just take it for granted, because I have way too much other stuff to do. But none of what I do is attempting to sell theological insurance, door-to-door, retail, or wholesale.

Ascending Acoma

So there I was ...

in the St. Esteban del Rey Church up on Acoma Pueblo, New Mexico. My younger daughter and I were visiting my elder daughter and her husband. It was Sunday, but there was not much interest in the group in finding the Quaker meeting that I knew was in town. The day was October, clear and crisp. I suggested we take a drive out to Acoma Pueblo, an hour's drive outside of Albuquerque. I had not been there in decades, but I knew the drive was beautiful, and I could enjoy my daughters' company and get them a history lesson at the same time.

We ended up on the walking tour through a village perched on a small Mesa that rises 367 vertical feet out of the desert. Our tour guide was Dale Sandoz, a matriarch of the Eagle Clan of the Acoma people. We were lucky to get Dale. She is small and round, "Like the cedar trees that grow at the base of the Mesa – strong, dry country growth." She splashes water on the ground from her canteen as a gift to Mother Earth, to secure a safe tour. The Acoma are matriarchal; all property passes from mother to the youngest daughter -- "Because we expect that she will outlive us all." A couple of long, tall Texas cowboys in our group discovered that you do not walk in front of an Acoma matriarch without being rebuked -- "But you ladies can walk wherever you like." Acoma governors are all men. "Women have more important things to do -- so we nominate them, and if they do good -- we keep them, if not, we don't." The village has been continually inhabited since at least 1150. The houses are two or three stories high, none have electricity or water. They are made of limestone blocks (the traditional material), or adobe, or cinderblock -- Dale regrets these innovations -- "But there are no zoning laws up here, and you can't tell a youngest daughter what to do with her house."

We started our tour in the church. It is huge -- at least three stories up from the plaster and dirt floor to the massive ponderosa pine beams that were carried many miles from Mount Taylor in 1629. "Because they were holy, they never once touched the ground between here and there. The men took turns carrying them, and rested them on platforms at night." The Spaniards gave them a bell as a peace offering -- and a peace offering was dearly needed because of the massacre of 1598. Thirteen Spanish soldiers tried to steal grain and were killed by the Acoma. One of them was a relative of the governor, Juan de Onate, and he retaliated with a brutal assault on the pueblo that saw the women taken as slaves, the men killed or left alive but with their right foot cut off, and children were pulled screaming out of hiding in the kiva -- their throats slashed and dragged through the village behind horses. The atrocity shocked even the Conquistadors, and Onate was eventually prosecuted. The Acoma were "given" a church. I'm not sure what "given" means when you spend a lifetime of the people -- 40 years -- building it yourself. The Acoma chose Saint Stephen for their patron. When they heard the story of the man who prayed as he was being stoned to death, "Lord, do not count this sin against them," they recognized him as their own. Dale says that they freely accepted the religion of their oppressors because they recognized the truth in it beyond the actions of its adherents. This woman is so **not** oppressed! She says that "99% of Acoma are Catholic and 100% practice the ancient religion -- because they are so similar." At the altar are four pillars carved from those ancient ponderosa -- carved as twisted, entwined beams of white and red, "For the two religions that are practiced here." Symbols of the people are painted on the walls of the church alongside paintings of saints and a prominent picture of purgatory. There are only a few pews up front to accommodate the elders -- the rest of the space is left free for dancing. A small window is aligned to admit a ray of sunlight to fall directly on the Santo only on the winter solstice. It is a most integrated place.

We walked out through the burial yard and through the village. I bought a small pot. I was deeply moved, but it took days for the full truth to sink in. The Acoma built that church twenty years before Quaker George Fox stood and preached for the first time. The Acoma had found Christ in the church of their murderers. They found a faith that spoke to their condition. They found "That of God' in the ugly other." They found a model for forgiveness in the worst of situations. We consider these to be Quaker testimonies. George would have had no truck with the Spanish Church; but he would have understood the Acoma.

One of those near the stoning of St. Stephan was the Apostle Paul – spiritually preserved, perhaps, by the prayer of his victim. Paul's image is also on the Acoma altar. I wonder if the prayers of the Acoma have saved Onate.

POMO Theology

There is a fairly broad consensus that our world is on the cusp of a new era. The modern world with its emphasis on reason, order, hierarchy and objectivity is being supplanted by a post modern vision of relationship, subjectivity, ambiguity and fluidity. Theology, never the most stable of the intellectual disciplines, is being greatly affected by this sea change. Like it or no, we will find new ways of understanding and explaining old truths or we will fail to pass them on. If I am any kind of theologian, I am a narrative theologian. I search and explain truth through story. It is a manner of practicing theology that I think is well suited for the coming age. The following columns are some of my attempts to transmit spiritual truth. They are a bit random. But random is very pomo.

Asking for Direction

So there I was ...

lost in Vancouver, Washington. This was during my itinerant days and I was on my way to preach the morning message at New Life Friends Church in the Rosemere neighborhood of a town that people often think is in Canada but is actually just across the Columbia River from Portland, Oregon.

Alivia Biko, my right hand, ministry partner, and musical director was not able to be with me that morning. I had grown accustomed to the luxury of Alivia, and one of the luxuries is that I almost never had to drive on preaching mornings. This is a good thing since I tend to go into a sort of unction fog an hour or two before the appointed time – it is not conducive to driving. Knowing that I would be thus handicapped, I allowed myself extra time, took the cell phone, plenty of coffee, and I made sure that I had a church directory for our group of Quakers. I thought I had things covered. I often forget whose job that is.

I was enjoying some liturgical music by U2 as I went north. BB King was singing "When Love Comes to Town" with Bono and the boys as I crossed the Columbia River. This is one of the greatest testimony songs in Christendom, I often have to open up the moon roof, or blessing window, as we call it, and raise a hand in affirmation when they get to this part

*"I was there when they crucified my Lord. I held the
scabbard when the soldier drew his sword.
I threw the dice when they pierced his side.
But I've seen love conquer the great divide."*
(When Love comes to town – Bono)

I may have seen Love conquer all, but I completely
spaced my exit. When I realized it, I just took the next
right and wound my way on down into old Vancouver,
trusting my sense of direction which usually serves me
pretty well, except on preaching mornings.

I was all turned around and I knew it. Nothing looked
familiar. I pulled over and consulted my directory.
Then I discovered my real problem. New Life Friends
was only six months old. I knew this because I preached
at their kick-off Sunday the previous November. This
meant that they weren't in the directory I was carrying
or in the local phone directory. I could not remember
the name of the street they were on. I had 30 minutes
to find them.

I prayed a bit and drove off in a direction I could no
longer identify, and then I saw my salvation: a cab
company. My definition of a town is a municipality big
enough to have a cab company. A city has multiple cab
companies. In towns the cabbies let you sit up front
with them, in fact, they are sort of insulted if you sit in
the back. I once had a cab driver in my home town of
Salem ask me if I thought my name was Trump – sittin'
in the back like that. I gave the excuse of having been
raised in Chicago and moved up front. Portland is a city
these days – you sit in the back, but they still don't lock
the front door, and there aren't usually bars or glass

between you and the cabbie. I wasn't sure if Vancouver was a town or a city, but I was glad to see that they had cabbies – because cabbies know everything.

I pulled into their yard and walked up to the dispatch building. A big guy in a loud shirt waved me on into the back room.

"What am I doing for you this morning', darlin'?" He said.

"I'm lost," said I.

"<u>No you aren't.</u>" He said with surprising vehemence.

"Well, I don't know where I'm going."

"Yes you do. You're goin' to church. Which one?"

"I'm preaching, at New Life Friends, in just a few minutes."

"Hmm...What's it look like?"

"Ummm, it's a little funky old place between a New Age bookstore and an espresso booth."

(*Note: in the Pacific Northwest, coffee addiction and New Age proclivities are pandemic. We sometimes have three coffee shops per intersection. The description I gave might have well as been "It's on a corner, next to a street.")*

"Ah, I know your place." He said confidently, and he gave me directions.

I was less than a mile away.

Out of the chain smoking mouths of cab dispatchers – once again - God's very own truth. There is no such thing as lost. Knowing where you are going, and knowing how you are going to get there are two different things. The knowledge doesn't have to be completely in your head. The reality is that I, and you, and the whole world, live in the palm of the hand of God and we couldn't walk off if we tried. When we step off, God's other hand is there to catch us like a Mr. Magoo cartoon. When we feel confused, we can always stop and ask for help, and help is out there.

Dispatch man walked me out to my car, and after I thanked him, he said this:

"Now, when you go in there this morning, - you're gonna be full of juice, you hear me? I'm tellin you, you're gonna Ace 'em. Just go Ace 'em Baby, OK?"

So I did.

Weirdness on Parade

So there I was ...

at the Galactic HQ of non-conformity, Berkeley, California. Visiting some friends, I was also taking in the annual "How Berkeley can you be?" Parade. Let me tell you, they have no trouble being extremely Berkeley down there. They have earned their adjectival status.

The parade included environmentalists and activists galore: local, regional, national, international, global and extraterrestrial. Many of them seemed to be anti-something: war, fur or government in general. But some were supporting things: creeks, the use of sign language, cheerleading.

There was the traditional nudity, despite the fact that the fall Sunday was crisp. I wasn't always sure what purpose this nakedness served. But the unadorned hermaphrodite made it clear that you weren't in Kansas, Dorothy. This individual was carrying a sign that read "Hermaphrodites for peace" – good thing, because they aren't letting you into the Army, honey.

There was a man in a bright pink unitard riding a unicycle. There was a Wiccan martini lounge orchestra. There are the faux groups (at least I think they were faux) like "Billionaires for Bush" – formally attired persons carrying signs that say, "Thanks for paying our share," "Taxes are not for everyone," and "Dick Cheney speaks for me."

There were art cars. A form of artistic expression that involves thousands of objects you have acquired at Goodwill and glued to your car. There was a camera car – early Brownie to digital, and cars covered in rubber animals, including a singing bass. There were a few Volkswagens in simple tie-dye paint – elegant and traditional.

One of my favorite moments was the convergence of a marching band of Klingon warriors with a battalion of Storm Troopers. The cognitive dissonance generated by having the Star Wars world mingling with the Star Trek world was phenomenal. The fact that these creatures were marching in this world did not even register on the radar of weirdness.

But the abiding moment for me did not occur on the street in front of me, it happened in the crowd next to me. At some point I became aware of a family on my right. Tie dyed mother and ponytailed father and their two small boys, one in a stroller. Mother and father were entranced with the spectacle, cheering each entry, and pointing out the nuances to their older son. This boy was about five, and he was taking in the whole thing. But his countenance did not mirror the joy and approval of his parents. He was watching this display of flagrant freedom with what looked like detached disdain. Not even the science fiction retinue piqued his interest. He thought these people were strange. He thought they were a little scary. The only words I heard him say were "Can we go home now?" I looked at him and saw a future Republican, a neo-con in the making.

Parents, take caution. It is easy in your enthusiasm to slip into an extremity that repels your children. It is easy in your oh-so-subtle indoctrination to fail to notice that your children think you are strange, or out of touch. It is important to tell them what you think, to transmit your values. But it is also important to ask them what they think, to let them speak to you. They may have some important observations. Listen to them.

Churches across the board in this pluralistic society have discovered that they have a common problem -- keeping the kids in the faith after they leave home. I suspect that some of the problem is the failure to attend to our own weirdness. A young man dating one of my daughters pointed out to me that you can tell a Christian song on the radio within seconds if it includes a reference to barnyard animals, usually sheep. He thinks the obsession with sheep is a little weird.

He is right.

No More Scapegoat Jesus

So there I was ...

facing the righteous indignation of an eight year old.

She stormed into the house, dramatically dropped her school bag and then slammed the door. My normally well-behaved and ebullient second grade daughter turned on me with eyes full of rage, nothing less than rage.

"What's the matter hon?"

"She held us after the bell! All of us!"

"Who? Did what?"

"The teacher. Ian and John were talking, but she punished us all! She made us stay after. **"She made us put our heads on our desks! I wasn't talking! I listen! She had no right to punish me!"**

I started a brief explanation of classroom management and why a teacher might try the admittedly lame tactic of using group pressure to control the few bad apples. Then I stopped. She was having none of it. She wasn't mad at the boys. She was furious with the misadministration of justice. I asked her if she wanted me to talk to the teacher. She wanted me to talk to the principal. She wanted me to get the teacher fired. She knew to her marrow that punishing the innocent for the sins of the guilty was injustice of cosmic proportions. She couldn't believe that they would let someone with such an obviously faulty moral compass teach children.

I knew right then that transmitting any semblance of Christianity to this child was going to be a challenge. Because sometime, someplace, some Sunday School teacher was going explain the core of the Christian message as this: You, little girl, along with everyone else, are guilty. God needs to punish somebody, because that is just how it is, somebody has to be punished. It doesn't really matter that you get the right person, so the Good News is that somebody really good, can step up and get punished in your place and then you get off Scot free. I knew this kid would be buying none of that.

Unfortunately I could not put the kid in stasis until I figured this one out. I started then to try and find different ways to talk about God, Jesus, and why death and resurrection are an important part of the story. It has taken me a couple of decades. The child is grown and gone. I am still working on it, I am not finished, but I have some handles.

The break for me started to come when I began to look seriously at the metaphors used for Christ. The most important one was this: "Behold, the Lamb that takes away the sins of the world." This phrase comes from the earliest explainers of the Christ story, the Apostles, those who knew Him, and those who sat at the feet of the first witnesses. They were all Jews. They were using a Jewish metaphor. The temple sacrifice, which was especially poignant for those who had witnessed the destruction of the temple in the year 70 -- the end of the animal sacrifice system. Jesus, they explained, was God's Lamb. Which brings us right back to "He was punished for your sins." Unless you go back and look carefully at the instructions for the temple rituals.

So I spent some time in the Pentateuch looking at the instructions. The sacrifices are all about community and restoring community. Bad behavior negatively effects community. Bad enough behavior breaks community. There is an element of justice, and even in the last resort, banishment from community. There is also a way to restore community. I discovered this when I found out the difference between the scapegoat and the lamb. Nobody talked much about the scape-goat in the church I grew up in. Once a year the priest was to do a ritual, in which all the sins of all the people were symbolically placed upon the back of a goat (unclean – not kosher – not part of the community) and the goat was pushed out the gates into the wilderness, presumably to meet a bad fate. What happened to the goat didn't really matter. The punishment was being sent away from the community. The sins got sent away, not the people.

The lamb was a whole different deal. The lamb was clean, kosher, spotless, good, and the lamb was not punished, the lamb was consumed. The lamb was fit to be eaten, fit to be taken in. The lamb was giving your best stuff to the community to show that your intention was to be restored. The lamb was about making amends, not escaping judgment. The lamb was taking responsibility. The lamb was investing in community.

Then the light bulb went on. I had been taught a scapegoat Jesus theology mislabeled as lamb theology. Jesus was the best God had, invested in us, not punished for us. Jesus was fit to be consumed, taken in, this was the message He himself taught at the last chance dinner. The Romans thought death was a punishment. God is not just a bigger badder Caesar. God understands that death is the universal human experience, and that joining us in even death is a connection of cosmic order. The ultimate community building experience.

But just wait one heretical minute! Did not Paul talk about "propitiation for our sins"? Yes, he did. I think Paul was spending way too much time hanging around with the Romans, I think it was starting to wear off on him.

So I don't believe in scapegoat Jesus anymore. I don't believe He was punished for my sins. I believe He taught me what to do about my sins, recognize them, send them away (i.e. stop) and then re-invest in community with my best stuff. Make my own amends wherever possible, and trust in the eternal resources that He made possible by joining my community to cover what I cannot. Come back, it works.

So what happened to the indignant little girl? She doesn't sit much under the teachers of orthodox Christendom. I think she is a Quaker in her heart, I know she is a friend of Jesus, she is earning her bread as a church secretary for the Lutherans, probably printing up those Lenten materials as we speak. But most tellingly, she is training to be a teacher.

Geek Squad Jesus

So there I was ...

inside an organ. The church organ was old even during my childhood. It had fallen upon hard times, having been sold with the building by the Lutherans to a small poor band of evangelicals. It was as big as a small house, from the motor in the basement that filled its mighty bellows to the 16 foot pipes soaring above the sanctuary. My mother played it every Sunday. Trained on piano she taught herself how to play the two keyboards and the extra keyboard of foot pedals. She had nearly perfect pitch and the organ that hadn't had proper maintenance in decades must have driven her to distraction. This is how my father came to be the organ's repairman.

He claimed it started with a toaster. She wanted to throw it out. He told her it was perfectly good, it just needed a little work. He was kinda cheap. She handed it to him. "Fine, fix it." So he took it apart and figured out what was wrong and fixed it. He was proud. She was cautiously impressed. She said, "You think you can fix anything, don't you?" He allowed as this might be close to the truth. She said, "Fine – fix my organ." And his career as a repairer of fine wooden tracker pipe organs began.

He climbed around inside that thing for years. And when there was occasionally something he wanted to reach in a space too small for an adult, he sent in one of us children. We learned obedience – touch this not that. Put your feet here not there. He was good with machines, and good with children. He was bold. And he knew that you couldn't fix the organ from the keyboard, you had to get inside it to do the job.

I cannot help the fact that he shaped my theological impressions. I wouldn't want to.

I have previously stated that I think that the death of Christ had nothing to do with punishment. Even Pilate knew that what was before him was a farce. So what did happen on that day outside of Jerusalem almost 2000 years ago?

I think something broken got fixed. I see Jesus the Redeemer, as Jesus the Repairman, Tech Support if you will. See, there was this system called "Time and Space" and running on this system was a program called "Humanity." And it got all buggy. And the code called "The Law" just wasn't working. So the system designer had to crack it all open. Get inside, wipe some stuff, patch other stuff, write some whole new stuff.

It's a frustrating job, but somebody's got to do it. It helps if the somebody doing the fixing knows what they are doing. It also helps to have patience. Sometimes, people are just dumb, they do not interface well with the program, and you have to very patiently explain to them, again and again, how the thing is supposed to work. But if the code is all glitchy, you have to get your hands dirty. And you can't fix the code from the desktop.

So for me the incarnation, life, teaching, death and resurrection of Christ is all part of the same repair job.

He got in, bringing with Him tools, skills, and a supremely solid connection to the designer. He ran the program, personally. Diagnostics were completed. One of the buggiest parts of the program was death, so he ran that too. But death was not the end, resurrection - the reboot to end all reboots was needed. Emptied the recycle bin called Hell while He was at it.

The Law was overwritten, the concept of clean and unclean wiped. Do you know what a time saver that was? Efficiency upgrade deluxe. Religious practice within the confines of tribal groups was made obsolete. Limitless grace was written in.

Then the lovely, fixed program had to be turned over to the users. So a help desk was established. Some people call it the Holy Spirit, some people call it the Present Christ, some people call it The Inner Light – there are lots of names for it. But it is there 24/7.

So we run the program. Seek the Kingdom. Pursue peace. Get serenity. Achieve enlightenment. War and hate are options under the free will part of the program. So are glory, sacrifice, and love. Calamity is just part of the set up. Calamity makes room for altruism and compassion. The whole thing works imperfectly, very imperfectly, but that is because of the human interface, not the program. The program works just fine. The human learning curve is steep but it is also part of the design.

Everybody in the program has a task. Finding it and performing it is the work of being human.

I am a minister of the Gospel of Jesus Christ. I work for tech support. I run tutorials. I coach new users. I scan for viruses. I help people with their upgrades. I try and keep a very solid connection. Occasionally I help people bust out of dead-end spots they get themselves into. It is a good gig. Frustrating at times, but very satisfying at others.

I come by it naturally. Dad would understand.

Jesus Gives Green Stamps

So there I was ...

at the Redemption Center. My arms cradled the stack of eight by eight inch newsprint books, pages warped by the spit that glued the seemingly infinite number of tiny green paper squares.

Mother had despaired of ever finding the time to empty the kitchen drawer of the logjam of paper scraps acquired as a mercantile bonus at the grocery, gas station, and department store. They were just slightly too valuable to toss, but rarely valuable enough to warrant the attention of my busy, creative mother. So she told me that if I did the pasting that I could benefit from the exchange. It took all of a Saturday afternoon, but in the end I had ten completed books of S and H Green Stamps. So it was with those vast riches that I entered the land of redemption.

At that time, any municipality worthy of the name had a Redemption Center where you could trade your books for goods. Honestly, I do not know how they covered the overhead. But in those magical places were rows and rows of shiny small home appliances, knick-knacks, sports equipment, baby supplies, and toys. Things that middle class mothers desired, but could not fit into their everyday budget. A store where you could buy without money. After an agonizing search, I left dragging a croquet set – fun for the whole family, and an act of altruism on my part.

But it must have been spring, near Easter, because I also remember sitting in church shortly thereafter trying to figure out what "Jesus, our Lord and Redeemer" had to do with Green Stamps. Life can be perplexing for children in religious families.

This memory wafted up recently while I was sitting in church singing, "I know that my redeemer lives," my favorite Easter hymn.

I've been to seminary; I am perplexed at a much higher level than I was as a child. I know that Redeemer is a Hebrew word. It does not appear in what we call the New Testament. The word never comes out of the mouth of Jesus or off of the pen of Paul.

The statement, "I know that my redeemer lives" comes instead from old father Job. The story of Job is considered to be one of the oldest stories in written human history. It is a story not just about suffering, but response to suffering – Job's response and the crummy responses of his "who needs friends like these" friends. Job's response is a stand of faith; faith in himself, in the God he is angry with, and in the scales of justice. He says, "I know that my redeemer lives and that I shall see Him." Job refuses to allow his friends to talk him out of his self-image of decency, and his belief in the decency of God, despite ample evidence to the contrary.

The only named example we have in scripture of a functioning redeemer is in the story of Ruth. The redeemer is the good man Boaz. Naomi, a righteous widow and her daughter-in-law Ruth, have through no fault of their own, come upon very hard times. Boaz is a near kinsman with adequate resources, and thus by religious law has the right, responsibility, and privilege to set things right. He does so, and has been remembered forever for his goodness.

It is for such a redeemer that Job hopes and waits. Job knows that his hope is beyond human resources, and eventually, God steps up.

I do not know who first made the connection and called Jesus Christ the redeemer. I have no argument with this. Christ, who by His birth became a near kinsman while keeping the resources of heaven, had and has the right, responsibility, and privilege of redeeming a world that has fallen upon hard times. He said his mission was to bring good news, bind and heal wounds, and set captives free.

But the teachings of Jesus Christ do make it clear that we are also to be redeemers. The Sermon on the Mount is all about using Heavenly resources to make things right in the world. That we are also to raise up and encourage the poor, protect the small, weak, and hurting, to set captives free. We are to be a blessing to this Earth not a curse – a force for justice. We understand that redemption comes through relationship, not through might.

We are near kinsmen to the children of Darfur, the poor of the world, the abused, the mentally ill, and the violent. We have the resources. We have the responsibility. We have the right. We have the example of the faith of Job, the actions of Boaz, the teachings of Christ. The world is our redemption center.

Jesus Fire Dancer

So there I was ...

enjoying the fire dancing. I am the pastor of a post-modern church, so my pastoral duties occasionally include things like fire dancing.

One of my folks invited me to come down to the Riverfront Park in our town and watch her spin about her head small flaming objects attached to chains. Some of her friends were dancing with sticks aflame at both ends, and the dancers were accompanied by a group of people banging on drums. All this was done after dark of course, on this cool, early April, Easter Vigil.

It was all very tribal, very pre-Christian, or maybe post-Christian. The dancers moved to the beat we all heard, but also to melodies heard only by their spiritual ears. The fires made great "whooshy" sounds as they whizzed about, describing circles in the dark air as if some wizard was teaching geometry to an unseen class. The circles got big, the circles got small, ellipsis and figure eights appeared around the dancers heads, feet and sometimes between their legs. The attitude of the dancers seemed serene, reflective, in control. Occasionally flames from one dancer would interact with the flames of another. I saw flames lick at clothing and hair but no one ignited themselves.

All in all it was a great Holy Saturday activity. I am a Quaker and one of our testimonies is that every day is a holy day and that all activities can be sacramental, but we are free to participate in all that leads us towards God, and the Easter Story certainly does that. I have long had a fascination with the Saturday piece of the story, called by some the "Harrowing of Hell." To harrow means to plow, or deeply disturb the earth; to disrupt the status quo.

It is clear that both the Apostles Peter and Paul believed that Christ was not inactive during the time between Friday afternoon and Sunday morning. In icons He is sometimes pictured as a preacher, speaking the truth to the souls in Sheol. Talk about a captive audience!

Sometimes he is pictured as a liberator bursting the gates of Hell open from the inside. Eastern Orthodox icons depict Hell as cold and empty with one or two chained demons and Jesus, resurrected, surrounded by former inmates. That's a great picture.

Hell exists. A place separate from God must exist for free will to mean anything, but the door is open and the exit sign is clearly marked. It is the church that has rebuilt the gates of Hell and found useful the scare tactic of inescapable torment.

While sitting in the dark and cold, contemplating Holy Saturday and watching neo-pagan fire dancers, I received a new image of Jesus - Fire Dancer. In my vision He shows up in the dark and cold of Hell and converses with the adversary:

a: Welcome. Always knew you'd end up here.

JC: Thanks, I make it everywhere eventually, you know.

a: Really? I think your traveling days are over bud.
Like the flames?

JC: Actually I do like the flames. Mind if I play a little?

He reaches down and picks up two handfuls of combustion and starts drawing circles in the air. A crowd appears. A drumbeat starts from somewhere deep. He steps lightly and playfully, showing His mastery, His serenity, His cool. The crowd starts dancing.

a: Cute tricks, been done before, but it's going to get old.

JC: Anybody ever done this?

The circle of flame above his head expands explosively, and He hurls it towards the gates. Those evil old doors crack and fly outward, and Jesus the fire dancer leads a parade out, up and away.

Hell's Freezing Over

So there I was ...

sitting at a lunch table with a group of insightful, visionary, powerful, spiritual women. We were talking about what it would take for our corner of the Body of Christ to embrace an application of our professed testimony of equality. Specifically, what it would take for the spiritual sea to change enough to make gender identity and sexual orientation non-obstacles to membership and ministry.

"What if we just opened that door and walked through it and let them watch? – Maybe they'd follow." I proposed.

"Yeah, when Hell freezes over!" said one of my sisters.

That phrase haunted me for a while after that. It rattled around in my heart like a marble in a glass milk bottle. Then the bottle broke, and it was spilt milk all over, but I had a jagged glass epiphany.

That is our job. That is precisely our job. We are supposed to be freezing Hell. Turning the thermostat of evil down till the devil is wearing thermal underwear.

Hell requires conflagration. Badness expends huge energy. Evil itches and requires lots of scratching, which leads to angry inflammation. Hellfire can be quenched.

The best way to chill inequality is to not participate in it, not cooperate with it, not ignore it. Racism is not by any means conquered in our world or our church. But in our country in the last century, it has been moderated by courageous people refusing to accept that it is the norm. Racism lives, but Jim Crow is history. People, a few people at first, just refused to be segregated, black people and white people. They just stopped participating. They had a chilling effect on evil.

We were created to be effective. Each one of us individually and all of us together.

Individually, we can douse and stomp on fires of evil that spark up around us. As a people of God we can be the cool soft rain that puts the forest fire to bed.

Hell loves a mob; especially a trauma crazed mob, an unthinking, angry mob. Hell especially loves an armed mob; guns are nice, but machetes will do. But it is amazing what a few people or even one person can do to a mob. Hell was having a picnic in My Lai, Vietnam when Hugh Thompson, Lawrence Colburn and Glenn Andreotta landed their helicopter between their comrades and their comrade's innocent prey. They stopped the carnage. The devil considered those guys to be party crashers. They were called traitors when they got home. Eventually, they were decorated as heroes.

What we don't know is how many similar atrocities, in that war, and in the wars since then, including the travesty of a conflict we are engaged in now, have been stopped short by one person saying, "Hey, that's not what we're here for" or "Don't even think about it."

They don't get written up as heroes for preventing evil. It happens all the time. The devil doesn't want you to know that he gets thwarted a thousand times for every time he succeeds in getting drunk on mayhem.

And don't think that it is only warriors who block disaster. I have seen a pig-tailed eight-year-old walk into a knot of bullies and take a scared six-year old by the hand and walk them out with a "Shame on you – I'm telling" look.

The truth is that evil is the sissy. Our spiritual adversary and all his minions are cowards of the first order. Hell can be frozen by the kindness of a child, the courage of a man, the voice of a boy, the persistence of an old woman. All we have to do is wake up, speak up, and step right in.

How I Became Invincible

So there I was ...

on the counter top considering taking refuge on top of the refrigerator. The initial screams of terror had given way to rapid shallow breathing. My eyes were dilated, my heart was pounding. My brain was sending out signals about imminent death. My adrenaline level was high enough that ripping through a wall to escape seemed sensible - anything - to get away from the nauseating, skin-crawling horror before me. I was Jackie Kennedy crawling over the back of that Cadillac. Oh, God, save me!

The mouse on the kitchen floor was perhaps two inches long, if you included the tail. My seven-year-old daughter was standing nearby laughing hysterically.

There were some parts of my brain that were fully aware of the stupidity of this whole scene. But those parts were totally trumped by my old brain. And my old brain was attempting to save me from a saber-toothed tiger.

Welcome to the world of phobias – fears that don't make sense. The problem here is that wires get crossed and the feeling of danger and the actual level of danger are severely mismatched. It can get you laughed at by children, but it isn't funny if your alarm bells are going off.

The old brain is arguably useful if there is a real, imminent, life threatening danger and the best answer is running or hitting. But for most of us, this situation is rare to the point of non-existent. Yet so many of us spend so much of our time afraid. And there are plenty of hucksters and worse who want you to feel afraid even when you don't need to because the old brain makes you very obedient. They want to make you phobic of life.

Actually, most of the time, we need our fancy new brain with all its reasoning capacities and creative problem solving abilities. When the old brain plays its trump card you lose everything that makes you human: reason, speech, altruism, relationships and the ability to pray – they all get thrown off the back of the wagon like granny's pump organ on the Oregon Trail – so much baggage.

But there's nothing you can do about it. It's automatic, right? Wrong!

I found out that my brain, even my old brain, is within my control. A brilliant guy* who trained me to listen to trauma survivors taught me this. Listening to detailed stories of rape, genocide, and torture is not fun. But I learned that I could be present to people in their horror without becoming horrified. I could be that resilient by choice and by a very simple procedure.

All I need to do is take a deep breath and soften and expand my abdominal muscles and pelvic floor muscles. It's harder work than it sounds, but if you can do this you can take the pressure off the vagus nerve at the base of the spine. That nerve is what sends the signals that tell the brain to panic. This procedure is the exact opposite of the gasp and clinching that we do when frightened. Anything that I receive thus – softly – cannot, will not, and does not hurt me. I practiced this for a few years and got really good at it in counseling sessions. I became very resilient; my burnout risk plummeted.

Then early this year I saw that smart guy again. He listened to my report and he said.

"Um, Peggy, you do know that you can do that all the time if you like, right?"

"What, just live soft? Like, all the time?"

"Uh, huh."

First I tried it on sometimes when my feeling of safety didn't match my real safety. It worked. It was work, but I could turn off my fear response if I wanted to. I did not have to face the ridicule of children, HA!

Then I waited for a chance to try it out in a setting of actual threat. I found I could quiet my old brain and keep all my capacities on-line. Present. Mindful. Dangerous instead of endangered.

Yea, though I walk through the Valley of the Shadow of Death, I shall not fear evil – Thou preparest a table for me in the midst of mine enemies. (Psalm 23)

You can't eat in a true panicked state. To have the table set in the middle of a battle is an amazing picture of how things are supposed to be for us. Relax, take a load off, eat.

If I forget, and I do sometimes, I can still get freaked, but I don't have to, and I can turn it off, if I want. If I don't take care of myself and sleep and eat and play, I lose some of my strength to do what I know I can do. But it is my choice.

I am resilient with the option of invincibility. It is what I was created to be.

For we are more than conquerors, through Him who loved us. (Romans 8:37)

I have always known this theologically. I am a child of God. I am safe when things are quiet. I am in the palm of God's hand when things are nutty. I am safe if you don't agree with me, if you don't like me, or even if you are actually out to get me. I am safe if I am dead because I am not my body and I live in God. I can choose to feel that foundational safety any time I choose.

For right now we are children of God, what we will yet become remains to be seen (I John 3:2)

So there I was... just a couple of months ago – in a pet shop – holding a rat in my hand – and I was laughing.

* With deep and abiding gratitude to God and Dr. J. Eric Gentry of Sarasota, Florida.

The Pillage of Wal*Mart

So there I was ...

looking at the news. Late in the day after the Feast of Gratitude. There was a video clip of two women being interviewed by a local TV reporter clearly at the low end of the reporting totem pole. It was this poor man's job to get a story out of how their shopping had gone. I almost clicked off, and then the camera caught an unusually good angle; the woman's chin up and out, a laugh rolling out of her mouth, and flash of her eye that meant victory. The look was one that in earlier times or other places would be called blood satiation. She had triumphed and was bringing home the trophies, scalps and booty. She had planned and executed an invasion. The God's and Goddesses of war had smiled upon her. She was the hero to whom the crowds yell, "Die Now! Die Now!" for nothing nobler could be achieved.

She had shopped well.

Oh, my sister. How we have fallen. This is our victory. The pillage of Wal*Mart. The plunder of Target. The sack of Sachs.

Clearly, no one has ever told you who you really are. What you were created to do. Let me try and give you a glimpse. See if it does not sound an echo within your soul.

Our most ancient stories tell us the truth of who we are and what we can do. In every culture, the stories exist.

Scheherezade knew these stories. Boudica told these stories to her daughters. These stories tell of heroic women: Judith and Xena. This archetypal woman has come down to our day and turns up as a blonde in Sunnydale. But she is here and she will not go away. You know these stories, you have just forgotten their meaning, and failed at their application.

The oldest story I know is of a garden. Firstmother was seduced by a lie. A fear-based lie. A myth of scarcity. She was told that her Creator was holding out on her. She bought the falsehood that she must acquire, by deceit or force, what she was not given. She realizes her mistake very quickly, but the adhesive gum of the price-sticker of that lie stuck to her soul and was passed down.

But not before her Creator gave her one more thing.

A task.

He spoke to her seducer and said this:

"You who were made for glory, you who has never had a predator, you have now made an enemy, and her name is woman, and you should be afraid, very afraid for although you will cut her, in the end, she will crush your head."

Not Firstfather. Not the second Adam who came to plant the new garden. No, **she** was tasked with vermin eradication. She shall have the final victory. Doubt me? Get thee to a Roman church; find the pretty Lady, the one of the serene face, the upturned eyes. Look at her feet, and see what is crushed under them.

Since that da, two forces have been competing for your soul my sister. One, a foul lie from Hell, which says that you are not complete, that you are not good enough, that you must have more, be more. The other force is deeper and more powerful, but often buried, unawakened. It says that you are more powerful than you could ever know – right now. That force knows that evil itself, fears **you**. You were meant to crush poverty. To thwart abuse. To free captives as well as to bind wounds. You were meant to have clear sight, wisdom, and power.

But sister, you have bought the lie. You have bought it wholesale, retail and on sale. You have stocked your cupboards with it and put it away for the winter. You have breast-fed and spoon fed it to your babies. Your soul has root cellars full of it.

You have let your enemy bind your feet so that you cannot stand your ground. You have let your enemy steal your right to read so that you may not look upon the truth. You have let your enemy impoverish you through mistaken wars you have enabled with your cooking pot and laundry pail. You have died bearing daughters who do not know who they are.

Yet in your deepest dreams the battle songs on Miriam and Deborah still sing.

Horses and chariots are no match for my God

There was nothing wrong with that feeling you felt on Friday night, my dear. You were hardwired to crave it, seek it, fight for it, and revel in it. But oh, my sister, my mother, my daughter, you have settled for a pale echo of the truth.

Give it a thought now, before we settle into the cookies and the glass balls and the laughter of children. And maybe on this New Year, you might want to sing a new song, and laugh a new laugh, and look your true enemy in the eye and let him see that you see him, clearly. Let him see that flash in your eye. Scare the Hell out of him, I tell you it will.

"Get the claymore out of the thatch where you hid it, Molly."

Veni… Vidi… Vi – effin – Ci

My Favorite Superpowers

So there I was ...

walking down the street with my four-year-old daughter. Well, actually, I was walking, she was running ahead – full tilt. I wasn't worried about her because she was a pretty well trained child, and I knew I could rein her in with my voice. I was just enjoying watching her move like every baby racehorse ever born. As she approached the corner I called out, "That's far enough, honey." She started her deceleration. Then she turned around, tiny hands on tiny hips and eyes of blue flame surrounded by a sunburst of yellow hair. She was clearly a little put out with me.

"Mommy, there is something I have to tell you."

"Ok, baby, what?"

"Someday, when I am running like that, I am just going to take off and start flying."

"Wow!"

"I thought you might be scared – so I am telling you."

"Thanks, hon, you're right, that might scare me."

"I'll be just fine, but if I am flying, I might not come back when you call."

"Thanks for the warning. You would come back eventually, wouldn't you?"

"Yes – I'll always come home for lunch."

"Great to know that – you gonna let me hold your hand to cross the street?"

"Yes."

I thought about this last week when I caught an episode of the new TV series "Heroes." It is the story of a group of regular people who suddenly discover that they have superpowers. A guy in Japan finds that he can stop time. A cheerleader finds out that she is indestructible. Another fellow discovers that both he and his brother can fly. The newly minted marvels don't know each other. They all think that they are unique. I don't know what they are going to do with this yet. Save the planet, I presume.

What an amazingly old story this is. Hercules old. Moses old. Buddha old. Shaolin, Shaman old. It is also new. Jedi new, Matrix new. I cannot think of a culture in which there is not a story line of mixed god/humans, or humans who attain a superhuman level of enlightenment and skills that go with it. The crux of the story is always what they do with the powers – save themselves, save the planet, or seduction and self-appropriation of the power to the destruction of themselves and others. Mr. Jung would have called the story archetypal, meaning hardwired into the human mind. I think it is so universal that it must be true. God has put into us a truth so strong that every four year old believes it. And even after we crush the literal possibility out of the minds of our children, it is a truth so strong that it oozes out of our consciousness every time we tell a tale.

We are meant to be so much more than we are.

John the beloved disciple, John of Patmos, writing a letter:

Beloved, we are even here and now God's children; it is not yet disclosed or made clear what we shall be, but we know that when He is manifested, we shall resemble and be like Him, for we shall see Him just as He really is .(1 John 3:2)

We have gotten immune to hearing "Everyone is a child of God", blah blah, metaphor, blah. John's ancient readers would not have heard it that way. They would have heard "Right now you are Hercules, what you are going to become can't even be described but will make him look like a sissy."

I have come to believe that this is true, that we are supposed to be superheroes. I have come to know this experientially. I am going to tell you about my top five favorite superpowers. You will probably dismiss this because it doesn't involve capes, and tights, and leaping tall buildings. You will say, "I don't want cheesy meta-phorical powers, I want a light saber, I want bullets to bounce off my chest." But I say to you, the light saber is the metaphor. These powers are real, they are available, and if you surrender to the Divine you will get your own set, and when you discipline yourself and learn their use, your life will be transformed.

Power #1

I have become frequently impervious to insult and offense. This was the first power that I discovered and so named. I was shown that just because someone is offensive, it does not mean that I have to be offended. I can choose, and offense is so rarely a good choice. Offense is a huge waster of time and emotional energy. I have much better uses for my time.

Power #2

I can forgive those who actually hurt me - the ones who do it accidentally and the ones who do it rather intentionally. This power breaks chains of bondage. It crushes walls of isolation. It allows me to move through regions that otherwise I would have banished myself from. It erases enemies. It short-circuits revenge. It stops wars.

Power #3

I have started to have what I call "Quixotic vision." Like the old Don from La Mancha, I have started to see people as God sees them. This is amazing. Some of the human trash of our society, the ones we warehouse, or worse abandon to the streets, are beautiful and saintly. Some of the most physically beautiful, smart, and powerful, are actually wizened, shrunken and deformed in their souls. The scariest part of this power is looking in the mirror.

Power #4

I can travel through time. Not kidding here. I am connected to a supernatural being that exists completely outside of time. Through that One, I can communicate and work in other places and times. So far, this is mostly through the work of prayer. I have prayed for my grandparents, I pray for my grandchildren who are not yet conceived. When I work with a person who was damaged as a child, I pray for the child they were, sending them strength and hope to arrive at the day of their healing. I pray for my own death. I believe that the universe changes when I pray. Not always the way I want it to change, but it changes.

Power #5

I am becoming hyper-resilient. One of my favorite story heroes is Buffy the Vampire Slayer. One of the cool things about Buffy is that she takes her hits but she heals fast. A good night's sleep after the worst day fighting evil, and she is back at it again. Me too. If I take care of myself, sleep good, eat right, escape to my fortress of solitude every so often, I do not run out of energy or hope. If I disconnect from my Divine power source through will or inattention, I fail. If I ignore the restorative spiritual disciplines, I might as well have a back pocket full of Kryptonite. I wilt. I whimper. I lose all my other powers. I screw up. I die.

So there you have it. I am "out" as a superhero. Deal.

But I leave you with another lesson from Buffy. At the series finale, Buffy and her friends defeat the ultimate evil by finding a way to break the Buffy-world rule that "once to every generation there comes a slayer." They elevate every potential slayer to full force, all at once. They kick evil butt. They unlock this truth – we are ALL supposed to be superheroes. There are infinite powers. There are infinite skill sets. Evil doesn't stand a chance.

Let's go save the planet.

It's still OK to hold hands when you cross the street.

Mythology

Some myths are true. I learned this from a cowboy poet who enlightened me to a whole genre called "Pert' near true stories." These are stories that while not historical in any natural sense are still so true that they ought to have happened, and should be told to educate young'uns and edify the rest of us. I know lots of those stories. Some of my favorites are in the Bible. But that is not what I am talking about here. Here is a brief collection of the kind of myth that just ain't so. A fabrication that gets repeated ad nauseum, often to the detriment of many, and still you can't stamp it out with a jackhammer. Here are three spiritual "urban myths."

The Myth of Scarcity

So there I was ...

twenty years ago this weekend, great with child. I was awaiting the birth of my second, and what would turn out to be my last, child. I was 28 and we had an almost five-year-old daughter named Emily. Five years of undiluted parental devotion had allowed this child to become confident, precocious, and fun to be around. We were confident of our parenting skills. I was not worried about birthing this new life. My husband had gotten a decent job with health benefits just in the nick of time. It seemed that all was well.

Nevertheless I was terrified. And it was a fear that I did not think I could say out loud. I did not know that anyone else had ever had this fear. I was afraid that it was impossible to love another child as much as I loved Emily.

Then Laura Joy Parsons arrived. I took one look at her and my maternal love instantaneously and miraculously doubled – just like that. Emily suffered no loss of love and Laura received all that she needed.

I have since found out that this is a very common fear of second time parents, but rarely a fear of third time parents. It is a miracle that sticks.

However, I think that this is an example of a larger and more pervasive fear-based belief system – the myth of scarcity. This myth says that there is never enough of anything to go around and you better get yours while you can and hoard it as long as you are able. This toxic belief creeps into every area of human existence and relationship. It shapes government policy, haunts people's dreams, and fuels competition in every arena. It says, "There is not enough love, money, happiness, fame, health, time, space, work … for everybody – so protect what you have and watch out for those other guys." It is the absolute proximate cause of all jealousy, envy, and most strife. It is the ranchers vs. the farmers. It is old immigrants vs. new immigrants. And it is absolutely, refutably, experientially **<u>false</u>**.

I will give three examples: resources, time and love.

There are enough resources in this world. Sure, we will run out of oil at some point. But until old Sol quits on us eons and eons from now there will be sources of energy; sun, wind, tides, hydrogen, fusion, etc. We will figure it out. There is enough food in this world – there is no excuse for a hungry child anywhere. There is enough work to do in this world. The reason that some do not have enough, and hear me – children in much of the world are truly deprived – is not because there is not enough to go around, it is because what there is, has been criminally distributed, and shamefully wasted. Communism is an attempt to address this criminal distribution. It has failed – not because it is a bad idea – but because the implementers, time after time, have been seduced by criminal greed. Capitalism says that if you rely on individual initiative and a free market that the distribution will be corrected by opportunity and philanthropy. Capitalism has also failed because its implementers have been seduced by criminal greed.

And criminal greed is almost always based in the myth of scarcity.

We hoard because we fear.

Hoarding is not God's way. The Hebrew children in the desert were given one day's manna in the desert – the stuff rotted if you tried to keep it overnight. Jesus prayed for "daily bread"; reinforcing this concept again and again. Don't worry about next week's bread, trust and work and it will come. God's way is to use what you need and share anything extra with someone else. There is enough.

One of the most nefarious incursions of the myth of scarcity into most of our lives is the belief that there is not enough time. That life itself is too short. We run at a frenetic pace and wail at the lack of the 25th hour and the eighth day. This belief rules many a life and ruins the quality of life. It is impossible to simultaneously savor and rush something.

The truth is that time is darn near infinite, at least from our perspective. Almost every faith teaches that you, or at least some part of you, is infinite, immortal. There is something else after this. We don't know or agree on what that something is, but most of us believe in it. And since this life includes the possibility of quality and meaning, there is no reason to believe that the some-thing out there will not be at least as productive, and meaningful. Our sensation of rushing time comes from bodies that age, and our propensity to chop time up into tiny bits, so that they seem to fly by.

What we do not have is the ability to do two things at once in any really qualitative fashion – this from a woman who can multi-task with the best of them. The truth is, I don't drive as well when using the phone, and drinking coffee, and listening to music. I don't pay as close attention to my loved ones when I am preoccupied. I do not have infinite choices. I have many choices, but I must choose how to spend my time. The responsibility flipside to the freedom of this choice is that I need to relax about the things that I do not choose and trust that the universe will take care of them. When I do this, when I concentrate on one good choice at a time, when I trust, then time slows down. I savor things, enjoy them, and remember them better too. There is enough time to do everything that I really need to do – because I do not need to do everything. I'm just not that important.

The most relationship-wrecking, and hence human-wrecking, application of the myth of scarcity is that there is not enough love to go around. We believe that if the object of our desire does not love us that no one ever will, so we get pathetic or controlling. We believe that our friend shouldn't really have other friends because that will in some way impoverish us. We believe that God is a worse parent than we are, and cannot love all of us equally. We buy into the lie that God has favorites – us, if we are arrogant in our fear – or them, if we are victimized in our fear.

The truth is that love is the most obviously infinite resource in this reality. It is renewable. It is multiplicative. It easily trumps death. People who lose a loved one grieve, but then they pick up and love again, without losing the love they had for the one who has gone on to another expression of life. Mothers and fathers love each of their children completely without robbing the others. If we believe that love is unlimited and time is unlimited, then there is no reason for jealousy. We are given these miracles to teach us about the truth of God's love. God's love is infinite and so is ours if we let it be. There is enough.

The Myth of Isolation

So there I was ...

lying in my childhood bed, terrified. I awoke with the
sense that something was very, very wrong. The light
was wrong. It was way too late in the morning for me to
be in bed on a school day. The normal sounds of our
household were absent. The teakettle had not whistled.
That is the sound that usually ended my dreams. The
sound of my parents sitting at the kitchen table reading
the scripture and praying for each of us children by
name had not occurred, that was my normal ten-
minute warning for getting up. I listened carefully;
there was not a sound in the house. Then I listened for
the sounds of the city. I was, after all, in Chicago, there
were millions of people out there. Then I realized that
the whole world had gone silent. There were no cars or
trucks rumbling down Harlem Avenue a block away.
There were no sounds from the neighbors. There were
no airplanes in the sky. A city of millions was silent.

I came swiftly to the only conclusion that a child of
Evangelical dispensationalists could come to. Jesus had
come like a thief in the night and had taken away every
good person from the world and I was alone in my
family, unraptured. I was scared but not really surprised. I wasn't all that good of a kid. But then I
thought about it some more and wondered if my little
brother might not still be sleeping in his bed. He was
kind of a pain in the neck, he might still be here. I
thought about how a couple of kids might try and
survive the apocalypse. I knew we were in for at least
seven years of tribulation. I wondered, if I forged a

note, would they let me get the folks' money out of the
bank before it was too late? I wondered if we could get
to our cousins, those people were Elvis worshippers and
had just found out how wrong they were – but it
seemed like taking up with heathens might be a bad
idea just at the moment. I eventually decided to go and
see if my brother was present. I left my room and saw
the silent, empty kitchen. The clock confirmed that it
was past time to leave for school. No doubt now. I crept
into the living room and to my utter shock and
amazement, there sat my dad. Looking out the window
at the two feet of snow that had fallen unexpectedly in
the night. No work, no school today. No trucks, no
airplanes. A city silenced by God, but not robbed by
God. I crawled into my dad's lap and breathed in the
relief of the pardoned sinner. I was not alone.

The fear of being alone, temporarily or permanently is
not just an irrational fear of religious children. The fear
of being alone is one of the most pervasive and destruc-
tive fears in our world. It touches almost everyone
eventually. It causes suicides. It fuels addictions. It
provokes people into crazy behaviors that increase
rather than decrease their chances of loneliness. And it
is a groundless fear. Because true isolation is a myth, an
impossibility.

Every major religion teaches this. Christendom in its
right mind teaches this. Jesus said, "I will never leave
you or forsake you, not until the end of time." The
Apostle told us that we are surrounded by a host of
witnesses cheering us on to finish our footrace. Angels
manifest at the oddest moments speaking the inevita-
ble "Fear not."

Science teaches this. We are all really connected. The wings of a butterfly can start a hurricane. There are resonances between particles at a distance.

The mistake comes when we use feelings to predict fact. Now I am all for feelings. Get the full 96-crayon box of them and use them as often as you can, but as predictors of fact, they are notoriously fallible. Sometimes we feel lonely. This is the feeling that defines a craving for more or better relationship. It hurts. It is supposed to. But if we sit in the lonely feeling and use it to predict an isolated future, and let that fear escalate, we will do nutty things. We will forsake our integrity. We will medicate our loneliness. We attempt to latch onto anything that seems to offer relief.

Loneliness is a feeling given to us by God to cause us to seek community. You may be unlucky in love, but community does not rely on luck. It relies on initiative. You have to get outside of yourself and your feelings and do something to connect. You have to give, and be vulnerable enough to let others give to you. It is hard work, but it works every time.

You commune with the past by living up to the investment that those who have loved you have made in you, and listening for their cheers from the stands. You commune with the future by investing in others and by tilling the soil and planting the seeds that will feed and shade those who will come after you. You live in anticipation of their gratitude, knowing that you will take your place in the spiritual mezzanine to watch their performances. You choose, by will, to live in the truth that you are a valued piece of a great company of saints. You take responsibility for your feelings and your life.

The fear mongers of this world and the spiritual realm would like you to live in the fear of isolation. They want you to predict, and then live in, the lie that you are likely to end up alone and scared. This will prevent you from making those healthy connections with the past, present, and future that foil the fear-based plans they have for controlling your present.

Let us reject this lie. We are not alone. We were not born alone. We were not alone before we were born and we will not be alone in our lives or our deaths and we will not be alone after our deaths. God is as close as your breath. The saints are as close as the ear of your soul. Community is as close as your outstretched hand.

The Myth of the Emo-link

So there I was ...

inviting attack.

Before me were a group of teenagers. Kids who had been expelled or dropped out from the local high school. Tough boys, a few pregnant girls. I was the guest speaker at a mandatory lecture at the alternative school.

My job was to leave them some tools to deal with abusive relationships. I have done this a hundred times in the last dozen years. It was a topic these kids knew as well as I did – probably better. They just hadn't found any solutions yet.

I always start with prediction and choices. If you can see what is coming next, you can sometimes step out of the way. This works, and it is usually where they are at. Victims or perps - and I always have both in the room - know what happens, but they lack models for dealing with it. They think victim and perp are the only two choices. So I give them other choices.

However, making new choices is still a form of reaction, not pro-action, or prevention, so that is why, if I have time, I always do a little exercise that spins their heads. I demonstrate, and so expose them, to the virus of invincibility.

It goes like this.

I start at the place in the talk where I explain that one of the predictors of an abuser is that they blame other people for their feelings and behaviors. And then I appear to take a little tangent.

"You know kids, nobody can 'make you' feel anything. You do know that right?" (They look confused.)

"No, seriously," I say, "You can be, if you choose, in control of your feelings. Nobody can make you angry, nobody can make you sad, unless you want to be."

They scoff, and without fail, one of them says, "My parents make me angry," or even better "I can make people angry" Oh, how I love that one.

"Really, son? You have that power – you can make people angry – just with your words?"

"Yep"

"OK," I say, acting surprised. "Let's try a little experiment."

"First, we need the blessings of the teachers." Then I make an amnesty deal where the young man will be allowed to use any words he likes, even the ones that get you detention, even the ones that get you expelled, for the length of the experiment." The room fills with tension – I have their undivided attention now – and they are rooting for their peer.

"OK, son. The feeling is "angry." You have one minute to say anything you like to me – **anything** – and try to make me feel the feeling 'angry.' I promise to be entirely truthful about what I feel. Go."

Now we find out how much nerve the young man really has. Some just bail right there. But many make a valiant effort. This boy did. He took a moment for observation and then went for what he thought was the weak spot of every female – looks. He detailed my physical imperfections. Not as brutally as he might, because I was standing as he sat, and slowly moving in closer, and staring him straight in the eyes with a smile on my face and this was starting to unnerve him. But oh, how he tried.

"One minute up." calls the teacher.

I report on my feelings.

"I am feeling slightly amused, and proud of you, young man. You showed courage, you gave it a good try. You didn't flinch. I respect that. I like you. I am not, however, in the least bit angry."

Then I ask the class if they can figure out why he failed. They are smart. They say things like "You had time to get ready." "You knew what was coming." "You set the thing up." but they come around to "You didn't want to be angry. You made up your mind that you weren't going to get angry."

"**Bingo**!" – It is one of the things that separates you and I from the critters. Kick the dog and he is going to snarl, or cower – perp or victim. But you and I have other choices. And I have been practicing, and I have gotten pretty good at picking what I am going to feel. At least when I am ready for it. And at that point about two out of ten think an entirely new thought – and the virus has taken.

I call this problem the Myth of Emotional Cause and Effect – or Emo-link. It is the mistaken idea that there is a mechanical linkage between other people's words and behaviors and our feelings and then our words and behaviors.

The tyranny of this myth is all around us. It is the thinking behind the notion of a 'crime of passion.' It ends relationships. It enslaves people. It starts wars.

The applications are legion:
I cannot control my lust, so you madam, need to cover up better.
I was afraid, so of course I had to lie.
He hurt me, so I had to hurt him back. I had no choice.
He cheated - I was so devastated, I just had to drink.
He/She/They were asking for it.
It is impact, not intent, that counts.

The lie is that there is a hard connection between the external world and your feelings. The truth is that there are default settings, and something like emotional cruise control, but that we can take our emotions off cruise anytime we want. This set up is necessary, it is smart, and it is God-designed. I mean really, it would be too much work to have to think it out every time. "Now, hmmm, what feeling shall I use here? – I have so many to choose from." It is efficient to have some default settings where certain feelings pop up in certain settings.

But default settings are set in childhood, and so many of our childhoods were severely faulty. The people who raised us didn't have much range, so we fall back on some pretty simple, often reptilian responses. Or they had all their wires crossed and then so do we. Or they had no governors on their motors and every little thing was **huge**. So we over-react.

If we are lucky, as adults we get the chance to learn how to reset our buttons. This is called healthy detachment. Buddhists tend to be much better at it than most Christians. We really should invite those folks over more often. They have the notion that you can do pain without suffering. The idea being that you can notice your pain, be honest about it, treat it if need be, but not make a federal case out of it. Spare the angst. Disengage the drama clutch, and leave it in neutral for a minute while you decide what to do. Just because people are offensive does not mean that I have to be offended. What a time-saver – that one is.

Booker T. Washington got it; he said, "I permit no man to narrow and degrade my soul by making me hate him."

It is Yoda, not the Three Stooges.

It works. It is efficient. It is anything but boring.

I recommend it to your attention.

Sometimes You Just Have to Say Something

Jesus said that if the people didn't praise Him that the rocks were liable to speak. The rocks these days might have a lot to say beyond praise. We know so much, we see so much of a world that is glorious and horrible, brilliant and moronic, toxic and resilient. Commentary does not always make things better, but sometimes it is just irresistible. It is my hope that my flapping on current events would not be just that – blather – but would provoke grace, in me and in others. I can hope.

Giving Women What They Deserve

So there I was ...

young, poor, and pregnant. This was ancient times and there were no in-home-pregnancy tests. You had to go see somebody. I didn't have my own doctor, or any insurance, so that left me to the free clinics and people who had agendas. I found my way to Planned Parenthood. I was a little nervous. They were kind. They were respectful. They gave me a test – I was pregnant. I was also days away from starting graduate school and I was waiting tables full time at a pizza joint to pay for school. It was about the worst possible timing. I was not happy. The doctor (nurse practitioners were unheard of in those days) could see my unhappiness. He sat with me for a few minutes. He listened to me. He made no judgments or suggestions. When my words and tears had run out, he asked me if I wanted to know about my options. I told him that my option was to be a mother, because aborting a healthy fetus did not fit into my faith, values, or ethics. He smiled and he said, "I think you will make a fine mother" and he told me where to get free pre-natal care, and about a program for free food for pregnant women, and where the free counselors worked. I was very grateful for his listening, concern, and advice. It helped.

Five years later, I had another unplanned pregnancy. Ironically I was getting ready to put the previous baby into kindergarten and re-start my education. Still, there were no at-home tests. I was still pretty poor. I was between health insurance plans. This time, due to hours and transportation issues, I went to a "Crisis Pregnancy

Center" near my home. There was no doctor; instead, nice Christian ladies staffed the center. They were happy to help me. They gave me a test. I was pregnant. I wasn't very happy this time either. The lady asked if my pregnancy was planned, I said no. She got really nervous. She started spilling statistics. She made some presumptions. I thanked her and tried to leave. She got more nervous. She tried to set up a video. I declined her offer, thanked her again, and got up to go. She actually blocked my way to the door and said, "I'm not supposed to let you leave without showing you "Silent Scream." I escaped. She yelled after me –"Please don't kill your baby!" I didn't, of course, and I also never got near those people again or the churches that supported them.

Eventually I did restart my education, earn a master's degree in Counseling Psychology at an evangelical Christian seminary, and raise two daughters. In my fifteen years as a pastor and counselor, I have walked many women through many difficult decisions including unplanned pregnancies, serious birth defects, and grief over pregnancies lost and ended. I have learned that the decision about whether, and when, to become a mother is never black and white and it is not one that women make frivolously.

This I believe. Every woman deserves a quiet, calm, unanxious, unbiased listener. Every woman deserves to know all her choices and every woman deserves to make her own choice free of coercion. She deserves to have her decision respected. She deserves to have her basic needs met, and this includes: safe housing, adequate nutrition, and affordable health care including contraception. We can afford this for every mother and every child. For me, this is a faith-based position.

Last week*, Mr. Warren Buffett pledged nearly forty billion dollars to help women and children around the world. Unbelievably, he is catching flak for this because of the possibility that about 1% of it will go to Planned Parenthood. I bet that Mr. Buffett is not too concerned about the flak – he seems like a self-validating sort of guy. So he probably won't be that impressed with my gratitude; but thanks Mr. B. I, like you, trust Melinda Gates – I also think she's smart. I think that the majority of the money should go to the third world – they need it more than we do. But I'm glad that a little bit will go to Planned Parenthood. They were there for me when I needed them. They did a good job. They listened to me, and respected my faith-based values better than the Christians did. I would send my daughters to them. Because of you, they will probably be there for my grand-daughters.

*July 2006

Boosterism Rules

So there I Was ...

having one of my regular conversations. There are certain situations that seem to occur with regularity in rather random places in my life. These situations tend to produce some regular conversations. I have learned to see them coming. I have learned to enjoy the permutations.

This week I was having regular conversation number seven: "I don't go to church, but I still think I am ok."

It is a good one. I know my part well, and I relish it. This conversation usually starts when someone finds out that I am a pastor. I think this often provokes in people a premonition of judgment. They apparently think that I will tell them that they need to think differently or live differently, or at the very least that I will try and get them to come to church. I don't know if this comes out of experience or not, but it is a predictable event for them. They pre-parry the expected thrust. They volunteer some form of information about how they don't go to church, or don't believe X, Y or Z, but yet they live morally, ethically, and feel pretty good about themselves. Then they step back and wait for my best attempt to poke holes in their defense.

So I don't.

My job is to tell them that I think that they are just swell. That if they were supposed to be in church, they would probably know that and that I think highly of them and that I am sure that God does too.

Sometimes this confuses them. Mostly they just relax a bit and then we can have some normal people time.

It's not that I think that everybody and everything is just hunky-dory, I don't suffer from any such illusions. But if they are not OK, they know it better than me, and do not need to be told. If they want to tell me about the not-OK parts they will eventually get around to it. It's not my job to provoke it.

This week's permutation was interesting.

A father of a friend of mine, a dignified gent of a certain age, flew out from the Midwest to spend some time with his daughter and grandchildren. I had been able to perform a small service or two for the family this year, and so I was invited out to dinner at a very nice place. A thing I don't like to miss.

While spending time on a restaurant waiting list that had Einsteinian time-bending capacity, we had a chance to chat. After he told me that he loved me, he told me that he hadn't been much of a churchgoer – that, in fact, he used to consider himself an atheist, but had recently considered softening that to agnostic. He told me that he had been deeply involved with the Rotarians and that he generally just tried to do the right thing. He waited to see if I was going to do any God-talk.

I was ready.

I told him how much I loved him. That the evidence of his good life was all around me in the faces of his family, and that I was sure that God didn't have any problems with him. Then we talked about the Cubs. Job done.

Then I went home that night and Wikipediaed Rotary International.

Here were my biases. It was boosterism, I was sure, based on one Kiwanis meeting I had spoke at early one morning, years ago – boy, those were terminally sunny morning people! I presumed that it was a dwindling group of post-war business people. I presumed that they would be Americans, mostly male and probably Republicans. I presumed that they were nice people – do-gooders, but probably not much of substance.

Boy, was I wrong – nothing new there.

There are 1.2 million Rotarians in 200 countries around the world. That's four Rotarians for every Quaker in the world. They are gender inclusive and inclusive of all religions. You can be gay and be a Rotarian. They are non-political. The Nazi's and the Soviets didn't like them and banned them – always good for the resume.

And get this! Since 1985 they have been responsible for vaccinating **two billion** children against polio. The Mother's Union approves.

When I was in Africa this year, there were kids in my household, they had not been vaccinated against any of the things that my children have no fear of – except one – Polio – that they were safe from. Now I know who to thank.

Like Quakers, Rotarians like to ask queries. This is their list of questions for deciding if a course of action is a good idea.

Is it the truth?

Is it fair to all concerned?

Will it build good will and better friendships?

Will it be beneficial to all concerned?

I want sincere Rotarians in charge of our foreign policy!

I know that they do not consider themselves religious in nature, but this would make a fine religion.

Dallas Willard says that the test of a good religion is its benefits to its non-adherents. I think this applies to all communities and organizations. I mean even the KKK has some benefits for its members. But the alphabetically superior AA benefits a lot of people beyond the drunks. By this measure, the Salvation Army and the

Union Gospel Mission are doing ok. The United States government, I am not so sure of.

Here's an idea. What if every Christian church that baptizes babies gave vaccinations with every baptism, worldwide. I am sure that the Mother's Union would approve of this. I am sure they could afford it; some of them have paid out more in lawsuits. Nevertheless, though benefiting billions, this would still be benefiting the adherents and so would lag behind the Rotarians.

I have decided that my friend's father does not need to check in with me, spiritually speaking. He has decades of good religious seniority on me, I need to keep checking in with him.

Loving Las Vegas

So there I was ...

getting my boots shined in McCarran International Airport, Las Vegas, Nevada. I was passing through with three hours to blow. The State of Nevada is, at times, difficult for me to enjoy. As a mental health professional and a volunteer fire-of-addictions fighter, the "Addictions R Us" atmosphere creeps me out a bit. I suspect that the blessing of Las Vegas is the feeling of normalcy for folks who may not always feel so normal at home in Des Moines. There are people there who will cheerfully help you hock your wedding ring to continue playing games, and do it as if this were perfectly normal behavior. There are people who will help you get married to someone you met yesterday, and act like this makes perfect sense. Women on stage wear enormous hats and not much else – no problem. Night and day have no differentiation. The party is endless – of course it is.

I was just passing through; I did not intend to join the party. I told myself that I would self-pamper by using the break to buy a good, relaxed meal. So I walked the concourse with anticipation, scoping out my choices. Alcohol – slots – slots – chocolate – greasy burgers – alcohol – slots – alcohol – Subway – slots: those were the choices. Subway appeared to be the top of the food chain. The most wholesome option was a flavored oxygen bar. Now, while I might wish that I could survive on peach flavored oxygen, I had been on one four-hour no food flight, and I had another one ahead of me. "Six inch turkey, please."

With two and a half hours yet to blow and still in the mood to be nice to myself, I looked for an opportunity. I am a collector of novel experiences, and when I spied a bored looking shoeshine man, I realized that warming one of those shoe thrones would add to my collection. My boots agreed.

The charming gentleman attending to my iguana skins was from Kenya. I had been to his homeland recently and we had a nice chat about Africa. Then I asked him how he felt about Las Vegas. He looked up at me, clearly deciding whether to give me the tourist bureau answer or the truth.

"The truth, please."

"I have a daughter in college at home and she is precious to me. So I am forced to love Las Vegas because I love my daughter."

I told him it was the best reason I had ever heard for loving Las Vegas.

Star-Belly Sneeches and Modern Day Cossacks

So there I was ...

walking the halls of democracy and sitting in the midst of hostility.

The Capitol Building of the State of Oregon is a short distance from my house. I had received a phone call from a clergyperson I associate with and she was trying to turn out bodies for a series of evening hearings at the Capitol. The legislature was considering two bills, one to limit discrimination against gays, lesbians, and trans-gendered people, and one to set up a way for the same people to legally protect their relationships in a manner akin, but not equal to, the institution of marriage. I could go, so I did.

My problem was that I was two weeks home from a Central African war zone. I still had a pretty bad case of the social/emotional/spiritual bends. It takes me about a month to re-adjust from the effects of genocide to the comforts and concerns of American life. I cannot do counseling during this time. I just cannot immediately work up compassion for normal American problems after being emotionally present to people living in actual Hell. I get over it. I reset all the dials. But it takes a while.

That night as I walked into the Capitol, I was not real enthusiastic. But I remembered that I normally felt quite strongly about this issue and I figured I could be bodily present, if not spiritually present.

The first thing I noticed as I entered was that everybody was labeled. It was Dr. Seuss and the star-bellied Sneeches. Everybody was wearing stickers to designate their side. There were folks in the doorway discerning what party you belonged to and handing you your sticker. I don't really like stickers on my person. I was picked out by the Basic Rights Oregon person and offered my progressive sticker. I was not real sure how I was spotted, but I declined out of sheer rebelliousness. The young man then took another look at me and spotted my grandmother's cross that I often wear around my neck. He actually took a step back, and said "Oh, sorry." That was my first clue.

The next thing I noticed was that the building was overflowing with people. I had trouble finding any of my friends. There was the main hearing room and then many overflow rooms with closed circuit TV and because those were all full, the lobbies were filled with chairs and people and additional TV sets. And security. Lots of security people. The security people looked nervous. Second clue.

By observing stickers, I noticed that all the gay families were huddled together in the hearing rooms. The lobbies were full of their opponents.

The next thing I noticed was that the people opposing the bills all looked like each other, really - they did. Round, scarved, middle aged women who looked like nesting dolls, and droves of tall, good-looking, clear skinned, brown haired blue-eyed men. A smattering of pretty blonde girls.

I found my clergy friend.

"Who are these people?" I asked.

"They are all from one church here in Salem. It's a Slavic fundamentalist church. They can turn out 300 bodies any time the pastor calls for it. Thanks for coming, Peggy."

"Where are your folks?"

"They are all together in the hearing rooms; nobody feels comfortable mingling."

Well then, that gave me my mission for the night. Mingle with the Slavic Christians and see what was what. I don't like fear-based segregation. I do not often find that it is based in reality. I like to challenge it and look for the good in the other side. That's my default setting.

There was a seat open in front of one of the TV's right in the middle of a knot of young men. I took the seat. The energy was really quite amazing. I could feel it in the air. Primal, like big sexual energy only about anger, not sex. Anger pheromones. I watched as people testified before the legislators - three pro, then three against. The rule for the evening, both in the hearing room and in the lobby, was no vocal demonstrations. But the young men around me were having a hard time containing it. Quietly cheering the people who predicted the fall of civilization if a couple of lesbians made a civil union, and jeering, hissing, and spitting invectives at anyone who disagreed with that analysis.

There were many dozens of testimonies that night. I got weary, but the young Slavic men did not. They seemed to gain steam from each chance to hate, which did not dissipate with the speakers who they supported. They had a one-sided reaction that ratcheted up with each round.

I was touched in some way by all the testimony. I was pretty put off by the fear-mongering, but when someone stood up and spoke eloquently on behalf of their alternative family, it warmed me, gave me hope, and trust that love would eventually win out. One young woman did an especially good job, and I just couldn't help but say a quiet "Amen, preach it sister." The young men on either side of me, sat bolt upright and looked at me.

"Hi, my name's Peggy, I'm with the other side – I just didn't get my sticker." I put out my hand to the young man on my left.

He did not take it.

The next speaker was a clergyman from some progressive protestant denomination. He wore a Roman-style collar. He spoke of God's love for all people. This really heated up my area. Much gasping and hissing. They really didn't like the pro-gay clergy guy.

The young man on my right sat with his fists and probably a few other body parts clenched. "Using God's name to defend an abomination! God should strike him dead," he hissed. I had the distinct impression that if

God didn't do it, that this young man would volunteer to be God's agent.

I suddenly remembered why I cared about this issue. These fine Christian folk, would, if they knew everything I believed and everything I preached, and if given a free rein, likely stone me dead without a second thought.

Think that couldn't happen in America? Quaker preacher Mary Dyer was hung in Boston Commons by fine Plymouth Rock, Thanksgiving Day, Christian folk. The framers of our constitution knew that well and attempted to prevent it from happening in the new union. But they knew it was a real problem that needed to be addressed.

 I remember something Garrison Keillor said about the Puritans, his forbearers. He said, "They came to America to practice religious persecution at a level not actually allowed under British law." He was right, the Puritans, of course, thought they were fleeing religious persecution and protecting their faith by hanging Quakers. The Slavic Christians gathered around me also fled religious persecution and believe that they are protecting their faith.

There was one other person sitting in that group that stood out even more than I. An orthodox Jew – side curls, hat, fringe – the whole thing. We don't see a lot of that in Salem. From his sticker I could see that he was in harmony with the Slavic Christians on this issue. When I got the chance I moved and sat by him.

"Hello, Friend, so you agree with these folks?" I said

"I do, they are on God's side of this issue." He said, stiff, not looking at me.

"Don't they remind you of anyone?"

"I do not know what you mean."

"Like, I don't know, Cossacks, maybe?"

"You do not know what you are talking about."

"Probably not, no, I'm sure I don't. But are you really sure that if they managed to put down the gays like they wish to, that they wouldn't come next for, oh, say the Jews?"

Then he looked at me.

"Just a thought." I said and I moved on.

A League of Extraordinary Gentlemen

So there I was ...

struggling with the hymns. You know what I mean; all I had to do was see the title after the worship leader called out the number, and a groan came up within me. "Not that old Clichéd rag! – oh spare me." Haunted hymns. Hymns I could only hear in voices that I no longer wanted to listen to. Voices that brought back so many fundamentalist memories that I had worked hard at putting outside the garden gate. Bloody hymns – lambs bleeding and dying at every turn. I had long ago given up the slaughterhouse metaphors as not relevant to my life.

But I was the speaker at this Christian retreat, and walking out of the room, while it would have been tolerated, would have caused concern among the brethren. And they were brethren. I was the only woman within shouting distance.

> "Blessed assurance, Jesus is mine! ...
> This is my story – This is my song
> Praising my Savior – all the day long."

George Beverly Shea, Billy Graham's worship leader always pronounced it stow-ree, and drawled it out nice and slow – it rhymed with glow-ree. I can't hear that song without hearing George. I tried to drag myself back from the stadium of thousands to the small circle of men. I looked at the present leader. He didn't look like George, he didn't sound like George. He was younger and lankier, and he sported a motorcycle jacket, soul patch, and some hipster eyewear. Boy did he have a story. A story that involved pretty severe, unwanted alienation from the people who loved him and whom he loved. A story that involved a stint in the summer camp for the criminally inclined that some people call prison. A story about Jesus, whom he just couldn't quit.

> "Oh, How I love Jesus ... the sweetest name on Earth
> It tells me what my Father hath
> in store for me every day
> And tho' I tread a darksome path,
> Yields sunshine all the way.
> Oh how I love Jesus, because He first loved me."

And then I am pulled from the present back to a hot summer camp meeting under the trees. Mosquitoes whining at the screens and nasal-voiced old women singing their love for their master. Those old women infected me with a virus of faith, and I caught their vision for preaching. But they didn't prepare me for the fact that they were sending me out into a world where many people would simply deny the fact that a female could have a genuine call to preaching the Gospel. I have sat more times than I wish to count with people who looked me in the eyes and said that I did not exist - that there was no such thing as a God-ordained female minister. The choices were delusional or liar. A very weird and discouraging situation. But not one of those folks ever told me that I could not be a Christian - that there was no such thing as a female Christian. The men sitting around me had lived through that level of denial. They are all gay men. And they are all Christians, but they have been told for most of their lives

246 SO THERE I WAS ...

that those two things are mutually exclusive. They have had their foundational reality rejected, again and again.

So I came and told them that each and every one of them was here on planet Earth on assignment from God, and that they needed all of themselves to stay on task. They needed to be integrated to do it. That their gender, their orientation, their history, or the opinions of the world had no power to stop them. They choose to believe me, because their very own spirits shouted that it was true. Music to their ears.

"Oh Lord, my God, when I in awesome wonder,
consider all the worlds Thy hands have made ...
Then sings my soul...
How great thou art!"

There are lots of kinds of worlds beyond and beside planets and galaxies. There are the infinite worlds that each human child co-creates with God by treading a path from the Eternal Heart, into a womb and a body and a time and a place and through a life and eventually back to God. We come into the world all but spiritually deaf and blind. With only echoes of glory stored in our souls. We walk through our childhoods, needing to be told who we are and what our purpose is. We need acceptance, encouragement, and nurture. We need example and model. We need the company of saints. We need comrades. We need a band of brothers.

But some of us get abuse and torment. Some of us get fed a steady diet of lies about who we are and our place. Some of us learn to hide rather than to shine. But against all odds, some of us believe anyway. Some of us keep looking. Some of us refuse to quit and die. Some of us keep seeking until we are found.

This is a persistent human story that causes awe among the watching angelic cohort who have never lived a moment without a direct connection to God, who have never been denied, never marginalized, never oppressed, never abused, never living a moment without knowing who they are and what they are supposed to do. We amaze them!

I looked around me and I saw 20 men – old and young, rich and poor, educated and not, white and blue collars, with challenges, with disabilities, with histories.

I saw heroes, survivors of trials, defeaters of lies, defenders of truth. Men with the superpowers of forgiveness, resilience, persistence, repentance, and recovery. Men who are taking up their tasks with courage and faith, determined to judge themselves only by the simple question of whether they were obedient to their assignment today. Applying grace to their failures. Determined to do as well or better tomorrow. Leaning to judge others – not at all.

And when, after the singing, after the scripture, after a lovely Quaker silence, after all the ancient, beautiful, bloody, broken words, they came around with the bread and the wine. Then the brother spoke to each brother, called each by name and said, "Child of God, this is the body and blood of Christ –**never** forget how much you are loved!" Then they came and said, "Sister Peggy, child of God, This is the body and blood of Christ, Never forget how much you are loved."

Once again I took Christ and Christ took me, in the presence of heroes and saints. I won't forget. And I heard the voices of angels singing "Holy, Holy, Holy," and saints singing

> "Brethren we have met to worship
> and adore the Lord our God.
> Will you pray with all your power
> while I try and preach the Word.
> All is vain unless the Spirit
> of the Holy One comes down.
> Brethren pray
> and Holy Manna will be scattered all around."

Holy Manna indeed, Thank-you brothers.

21st Century Pharaoh

So there I was ...

sitting by the side of the road waiting for my speeding ticket. I was half way between Portland and Boise and you know, there are some real lonely stretches out there. The day was clear and fine and dry. The sheriff's deputy was sitting at the bottom of a long downward slope, behind an overpass support. I got nabbed. I tried to argue that I was not being unsafe, that I was at a reasonable speed for the conditions. I tried to smile and "Yes sir" my way to the warning. He was having none of it. I was "In excess of the legal limit." And the limits were not moving that day for me. Reality check time.

I was thinking about this today when I read some comments by the Rev. Creflo Augustus Dollar Jr. of College Park, Georgia.   Apparently a United States senator has decided to investigate the finances of TV preachers. It would seem that this statesman has gotten bored with shooting fish in a barrel, but is not quite up to the job of taking on Blackwater or some other less obvious miscreants.

Creflo, and his wife Taffi, (Is this a Georgia thing or do these people have cartoon character names?) lead a church that takes in 69 million dollars a year. We are told that they live an extremely extravagant lifestyle. We are somehow not surprised. But Rev. Dollar takes offense at the investigation and defends himself by saying that his lifestyle is supported by personal funds from capitalistic ventures and not church money. The Dollars (rather redundantly) preach and live a prosperity doctrine. God wants you to be rich – just like us. See how much God loves us? Speaking about his standard of living, Creflo Dollar had this to say:

"Just because it's excessive, doesn't mean it's wrong."

First off, Creflo, buy a dictionary. According to the Merriam Webster online dictionary, excessive is defined as "Exceeding the usual, proper, necessary or normal." Its synonyms are immoderate and inordinate. You might want to look those up too. Excessive does mean it's wrong.

Secondly, when we hear "Too much is never enough" out of Mick Jagger's excessive lips, we are not shocked. But when we hear the same sentiment from a guy who claims to represent Jesus, it is a bit hard to take. Maybe the Sermon on the Mount fell out of the Reverend's Bible, but mine talks about simplicity and humility. The Jesus of my Bible tells ministers not to bother with an extra coat. Rev Dollar has extra jet airplanes. My Jesus is pretty concerned with the "Least of these." I am sure that the Reverend Dollar could quote me plenty of prosperity proof texts, so I think I will come at this from an angle I bet he understands – math.

Creflo, when you defend your standard of living, when you say that it is what God wants for everyone, there is just one problem. The numbers don't crunch. A few people can live like you do only if millions live at a much lower level and yet consistently pump resources upwards towards the few on top, and those millions can only do that if hundreds of millions of others live in destitution. You get the middle millions to pump money upwards by promising them that if they do, that they will have the chance to be one of the few at the top, or at least near the top. You know what we call this? It is called a pyramid scheme.

Pyramid schemes can only be built by lying about the total quantity of resources. Pyramid schemes need a constantly increasing number of suckers to fill the lower ranks. Pyramid schemes always crumble, but not before the very few at the top make out like bandits.

It does not matter whether your riches come through the channel of the church or the church of secular greed. Your lifestyle is still supported by the middle classes and the masses of poor below them.

Now I am not saying that Mother Earth cannot support her children. I am not saying that there are not enough resources for everyone to live a decent life. Actually, there are. The problem is that your life is not decent – it is, in fact, extremely indecent. Your excess directly robs the poor of their hope for decency.

Frankly, I do not have much hope for any improvement in this situation at the investigative hands of Senators with lifetime incomes, and guaranteed permanent health care who cannot manage to make health care accessible to our nation's children. Pots and kettles to you, Mr. Senator

I do have hope in the One who told the rich young ruler to go and sell his goods and feed the poor. And I have hope in those who can still read His words with understanding.

A Very Practical Man

So there I was ...

watching "The City that Works" work.

I grew up on the edge of Chicago. Much to my mother's dismay, I had a profound interest in politics. Late in adolescence I wrangled an entry level job in the office of the 44th Ward Alderman, the Honorable Dick Simpson. Mr. Simpson was one of the two aldermen in the city who did not belong to what was lovingly referred to as the "Daley Machine." Richard J. Daley – Richard the first, as he is now named - was in the waning years of his power, but that power was so immense that the waning was not much noticeable. This regime is considered by many to be one of the most corrupt oligarchies ever to exist in America. It was also one of the most stable.

Because it worked. The snow got plowed, the garbage got picked up, the river got dyed green every St. Patrick's day without fail. People knew what to do to get their problems fixed. The regime failed certain groups of people rather badly, but they were, after all, minorities. The majorities knew that a certain level of corruption was tolerated, but as long as the garbage got picked up, they did not seem to care.

I got to watch the workings of the City Council from a slightly closer vantage point than the average citizen. Because I was a pup, and a girl to boot, no one paid any attention to me. I watched and listened. The first surprise that I absorbed was that by and large, these men were not evil. With a couple of notable exceptions they appeared to be sane. Many of them considered themselves to be religious men. They certainly considered themselves to be practical men. This was their bottom line. They absolutely believed that the ends justified the means. They did not usually say that out loud, of course, because when I was a child, society still nominally agreed to general moral truths, and most children could have told you that the "right" answer was that the ends did **not** justify the means. But the right answer was not the practiced belief of that oligarchy.

We are presently witnessing the waning days of a president who considers himself to be a practical man. He considers himself to be a religious man. And surprisingly, he is slightly more transparent than the pols of my youth. The other day, he stood up there on the porch of that stately old house and said approximately this:

I know y'all don't like torture. I don't like torture. But we need to keep it in the tool box, 'cause sometimes it is the only practical tool for the job. My job is to keep all y'all safe from the bad guys, and the bad guys are bad, and they want to hurt y'all. And sometimes the only way I can stop them is to let my boys hurt them first. It's not nice, but it is practical.

He only got this honest when push came to congressional shove. He had been saying for a long time that we never used this tool, and didn't have this tool.

Thank-you, Mr. President for the last ditch transparency.

I wish the president had gone one step farther, and given us a similar spiritual transparency. Something like this:

I know y'all like Jesus. I like Jesus. I talk to Jesus. But Jesus was never president. Bein' president is a hard job. The stuff that Jesus said is just not practical. Not for dealing with these bad guys and keeping y'all safe.

I think the president also believes that most people, when it came down to it, would agree with him. That torturing "bad" people to save the lives of "innocent" people is ugly, but perhaps necessary. Maybe he is right. I hope not. But it is the natural and logical result of a nation that believes that war is sometimes justified. After all, if you can sometimes honorably kill people on the field of battle, then doing something less than killing them off the battle field for the purpose of saving civilian lives is certainly the lesser evil.

The only person I can speak for is myself. This I say. Please, do not torture anyone to save my life. Do not torture anyone to save the lives of those I love – that includes my children, I do not think they would disagree.

I believe that the means are more important than the ends. I am going to die. Everyone I love is going to die. I accept that. But I believe that I am safe in my life now, and that I will be safe in the hands of God when I die – regardless of how that death comes to me.

If you can prolong lives by promoting justice, and thwarting evil, please do so. You have my permission to capture, interrogate, charge, and put on trial anyone you suspect of plotting evil. You may, with my permission, use any method that the police department here in Salem, Oregon, could use on me, if they suspected me of plotting evil. But not one right more than they have. And yes, I accept the consequences of that.

I have had another life experience that most Americans have not had. I have met, worked with, learned to deeply respect, and earned the respect of, torture survivors. I have done this in both the US and in Africa. I have also listened to young American veterans, ones who have implemented your practical policy. They tell me that the "spooks" (the CIA) do not like to do the work themselves, and often delegate the actual implementation to whatever enlisted person is nearby. I have learned that torturer and tortured are both gravely damaged in the process. The long-term damage to society is far more expensive than the obscenely expensive wars that we commit in the name of practicality. The legacy of the present regime will be costly in ways we cannot quantify or qualify.

I believe that the means of Jesus are eminently practical, and get results as good as or better than your means. I believe that that the simple, secular ethics that our country was founded on are practical. Dick Simpson taught me this. Do the right thing. Let the chips fall where they may. It will work just as well as the practical corruption that surrounds you.

Written in March 2008

Poll watching

So there I was ...

poll watching in the 44th Ward of the City of Chicago, 1975. I was a youthful volunteer in the office of Alderman Richard Simpson. I wasn't old enough to vote but I was bright enough to poll watch. Poll watching was a tradition necessitated by corruption.

The voting machines were those big mechanical monsters with the levers that clicked and the Las Vegas style side arm that swept your vote into the count with that satisfying "Ka-chunk." At the end of the day, a human had to open up the machine and look in the back and call out the numbers. Another human wrote the number down as they were called out, another human carried the book downtown where more humans tallied the numbers from the books.

And at each step of the way, we assigned a human to watch the official human. Did he call out the number that was there? Did he write down the number that was called out? Did that book stop anywhere between the precinct and city hall? At each step, corruption had its chance, and at each step we watched them. It worked pretty well as long as you had an army of volunteers. This was quite an education for a young, optimistic kid interested in politics.

City hall was a trip in those days. All the aldermen were men, and they were all white. Few of the staffers were female, and fewer still youngsters, but somehow I had the run of the place. The rooms of city hall were blue and brown with cigarette and cigar haze; the former tended to float above the latter. They had a thirty-gallon coffee urn, and they made the coffee on Monday and re-heated it all week. Friday coffee dissolved metal. You got tough or croaked.

The guy I worked for lost almost every vote 48-2, but he knew he was right so it didn't matter. Wrigley Field was in the 44th, and on a sunny, summer day (pre-lights at Wrigley) nobody cared if you took the afternoon off and took in a game. All in all it was a sweet deal.

I learned to take corruption as part of the package. There was a precinct in the city that was nothing but a mom and pop store and a cemetery, but that precinct turned out a large vote every time the Mayor was up for election. The bums loved Election Day; voting for whiskey kept them busy all day long.

But I also learned that you could deal with corruption - you could witness to it - you could moderate it. Some days you could even talk to it and get stuff done.

The ironic truth was that while Dick Simpson may have needed poll watchers to get his votes counted, the Mayor never needed corruption to get his. Cook County Illinois may have stolen the 1960 election for JFK, but the people of the City of Chicago loved Mayor Daley; he won by an honest landslide every time. The garbage got picked up, the snow got plowed, and everybody knew the rules. You were taught the rules.

My driver's education teacher stood before our class and showed us how to fold a ten dollar bill behind our driver's license in just the right way and then to present the whole wallet to the cop.

"Never, I mean never, offer a cop a bribe," He said. "That's wrong and it's stupid - cops don't like to have their integrity questioned. Put the bill behind your license like this. If he wants it, he will take it, if he doesn't, he will take your license and hand you back the wallet. Nobody wants some snot-nosed kid calling you crooked."

I also learned about political delusion, a thing running rampant in our nation's capital these days. Daley was getting old when I was there. He was fat. He was Irish. He smoked. He was red in the face all the time. It was only a matter of time until he fell over from a heart attack. And the city of seven million had absolutely no plan for succession.

 One day, an alderman stood up in city council and said, with great respect and humility, "Meanin' no disrespect to da mare, may he live to be a hunnert, but don'cha suppose we need ta, maybe, just in case, have a plan, you know, if, God forbid, something should happen ta him, a long, long time from now?"

Stunned silence ensued.

And then, Vito Marzullo, 25th ward, rose to his feet, and shouted at the top of his lungs;

"Our Mare, Richard J. Daley, mare of the great city of Chicago, WILL NEVER DIE!"

And that ended that discussion. Alderman Marzullo was, of course, incorrect in his assertion, Daley died a few years later, and it was a mess.

I have been thinking a lot about the oligarchy that was Chicago, and how much they loved voting. They loved it like they loved baseball. They loved it like they loved food and beer. Politics was the religion of the city as much as Catholicism. Looking back, both politics and Catholicism were probably corrupt, but back then nobody cared. People came from places where their grandparents' votes and prayers weren't counted.

I have been thinking about my friends in the Democratic Republic of the Congo. They voted last week*. For many citizens this is their very first taste of democracy. They are still waiting for results. The United Nations poll watchers report that despite incidents of violence and corruption, the election proceeded with enough integrity that it should count.

I am sure that they have relaxed their standards. But what people there are hoping for, dreaming for, is the kind of election that Chicago, America, takes for granted - one where the loser admits that he has lost, and does not immediately start an armed insurrection. Mr. Kabila and Mr. Bemba have both said they will respect the results, but they both have armies, and folks are worried.

What the people of the Congo need is for the loser to lose, and then the winner to actually form a government that works, most of the time; well, some of the time would be a good start. They don't have any snow to shovel, but they need some roads, and some police. Police who would only sometimes take the bribe would be a great start. At the moment, they only sometimes have police, and the police sometimes rape and kill. A democratically elected, predictable, stable, oligarchy would be a great improvement for my friends - like it was for Chicago in the 20th century.

I respectfully submit that Chicago should send a delegation to help. Experience, a track record of success, and karmic debt should determine the members. I nominate Fast Eddie Vrdolyak, Vito Marzullo and Dan Rostenkowski for point men.

Out of gratitude I am sure that the DRC would be glad to send us some great musicians, a thing Chicago also loves. Everybody benefits, everybody's happy.

Now go out and vote! Once!

PS: Please do not write and tell me that Vito is dead. This I know. This has never yet stopped a Chicago politician.

fall 2008

2009 – It could be argued that Rod Blagojevich should be added to the delegation. He certainly meets the karma criteria, but I think that he fails in the success department. He is such a punk that I wouldn't inflict him upon the people of the Congo.

The End

I wrote 100 of these columns for UPI between January 2006 and March of 2008. If you have made it this far, you have read 59 of them. I am grateful to God for the opportunity and for the discipline of weekly deadlines. The "So There I Was" format still feels useful to me. I have written a few others for my blog since finishing with UPI, and I will probably continue to do so. I am gathering all the stories from my Africa travels into a companion volume that you can expect to see fairly soon. But for now; how I ended it with United Press International.

Exit Stage Left

So there I was ...

playing one more game of Spider Solitaire on a rather unremarkable Friday afternoon in January 2006. I don't always open e-mails that start with Fwd:Fwd. But this one came from a good friend, and I was kinda bored. The missive was a general call for writings on spirituality. United Press International was starting a religion and spirituality page and was looking for a stable of writers from a broad spectrum of faiths, practices, and spiritualities to write weekly columns. Oddly, I had already toyed with writing in a newspaper column format and had a couple of samples already in the can. I sent off two of my favorites along with the requested bio to some fellow named Larry Moffitt. Within hours, I had a response and an agreement.

Some people think that I have a bit of a Superman complex, but actually, I have always had a crush on Jimmy Olson – cub reporter. I loved the bustle of the newsroom. The shouts of "Hold the presses!" I am old enough to remember actual newsboys hawking papers between lines of traffic and on busy corners. I remember when newspapers came out more than once a day. I remember when any city worthy of the name had **three** daily papers. As soon as I could read a paper, I was reading Mike Royko and Bob Greene in the Chicago Daily News and the Sun Times. You have no idea how much I miss Mike Royko.

My first experience writing for a weekly was in eighth grade. I wrote the humor page on that purple mimeographed rag. I also was the first writer to cause that paper to be confiscated by the authorities for the crime of mocking a math teacher. I managed to keep one copy hidden and have it tucked away to this day. I don't actually think the math teacher was too offended, until the other teachers told her that smart-alec students shouldn't be given so much rope.

Here, many decades later, I wondered how much rope I was going to get from UPI.

A couple days after I wrote my first column I was really starting to appreciate my editor Larry. He seemed to be a real mensch. He was a light editor. He left me my voice. He let me get away with some pretty non-standard sentences. He let me noun my verbs. He also let me verb my nouns. I liked him right away. So I googled him. That is when I found out that UPI had been purchased in the late nineties by the Unification Church, Rev. Moon's Church, and that Larry Moffitt was well placed in that organization. This caused me to do some pretty sincere thinking.

But rocks and glass churches certainly seemed to apply. I had recently taken to the renegade trail off of a sect of Christendom that itself was branded heretical at the get-go, 350 years ago. So I decided to test the promise of the Religion and Spirituality page and its progenitor. He said that he would not edit for content. He said that you could narrowcast to your heart's delight. He said that he was trying to get as broad a spectrum as possible. Turns out - he is an honest man.

I wrote my heart out for this effort. I wrote from a place of expectant listening to the Divine. I pushed all the imagined boundaries – they all flexed. I read the columns of my fellows. What an amazing bunch of humans. Some of them regularly bring tears to my eyes. Some of them torque me off without fail. I respectfully and cheerfully hope that I torque some of them off too. This stable of writers not only has a left end, it has a left field. My kinda town.

One of my favorite moments in this process was the day I discovered that the editor of a solid mid-western conservative Quaker magazine had liked one of my bits and wanted to publish it. Being a pro, she contacted Larry for permission. If you had predicted, even a few months before this, that at some point in the future, the stars would align in such a fashion that the editor of Quaker Life would be speaking to a ranking member of the Unification Church seeking permission to use **my** words, I would have peed my pants laughing. And yet this is what happened. Do not tell me that God does not have a wacky sense of humor and a love of street theatre.

When I went to Africa last year,(2007) I went as a freelance journalist, religious stringer for UPI. At the end of my trip I ventured into the Democratic Republic of the Congo, an active war zone prone to earthquakes and sudden volcanic activity. I needed to do this without escort or translator and it was going to be a bit dicey. I decided not to worry my loved ones, and sent my proposed itinerary to Larry Moffitt. I was pretty sure that he didn't actually have to power the pull me out of a disaster, but I thought he might have the phone numbers of a few people who did. It may have been delusional, but I felt safer because he knew where I was.

I suspect that there are not many things on which the writers and editors of this forum could all agree. But I can name a few of those things. We believe in speaking honestly. We believe in listening respectfully. And maybe, just maybe, we believe in peace through tolerance. This would be the notion that broadcasting all voices produces a better result than attempting to silence some voices.

I am deeply grateful for the opportunity, the acquaintances, and the associations.

But with respect, I now follow old Helen Thomas, and gracefully exit, stage left.

You can find the religion and spirituality forum at http://www.religionandspirituality.com/

About The Author

Peg ... yeah ... God's very own loose cannon.
Derek Lamson, musician, Portland, Oregon

Here she is - the woman who puts the rev in Reverend...
Gwen, Methodist pastor, Salem, Oregon

The pastor that won't go out to pasture.
Tom Smith, Ohio

Of course it's nothing we haven't heard before, but she
does it very nicely. Unnamed Church Secretary

The kick in the teeth that Quaker spirituality is asking
for. Mike España-McGeehon, Newberg, Oregon

Not a morning person but awesome after a few cups of
coffee. Ashley Wilcox, Seattle

Margaret Fell in leathers and crash helmet!
T. Vail Palmer Jr., Albany, Oregon

I'm glad she didn't go over to the dark side of the Force.
Gregg Koskela, pastor, Newberg Friends

She'll kick all your excuses to the kerb - with some very
fancy boots! Gil Skidmore, Reading, England

Peggy makes radically thought-provoking points with personal stories that *sing*. Nate Swift, Medford, Oregon

Peggy adeptly walks the thin line between sacrilege and prophesy. Liz Oppenheimer, Minnesota

Man, she gets cranky when she can't find her keys. Laura Holman, daughter #2, Salem

Before reading Peggy's blog, I did not know how to play the saxophone. But Peggy showed me the way: you've got to put down the ducky. Dave Carl, Arkansas

No namby-pamby wishy-washiness here. "Rantwoman" Dorene C., Seattle

Peggy describes herself as a motorcycling Quaker preacher, counselor, teacher, and free lance provocateur of grace. Her blog can be found at sillypoorgospel.blogspot.com. She also invites you to visit the website of Freedom Friends Church at freedomfriends.org. You can find out how to contact her there.